D0861100

ANNULMENTS

Fifth Edition Revised

Lawrence G. Wrenn

Canon Law Society of America
Washington, D.C. 20064

Copyright 1988 by Canon Law Society of America
First edition copyrighted 1970. Second edition 1972.
Third edition 1978. Fourth edition 1983.
All rights reserved
ISBN: 0-943616-42-5
SAN: 237-6296

Qui potest capere capiat

Mt. 19, 12

CONTENTS

Preface

PREFACE

This fifth edition differs from the fourth in several ways, of which the following seem to be the most notable. First of all, throughout this edition the CLSA translation of the Code is used (the fourth edition, which was published prior to the CLSA translation, used an earlier draft which was not nearly as good). Another outside source that influenced this fifth edition is the revision of the third edition of the *Diagnostic and Statistical Manual of Mental Disorders* (DSM III R). Wherever appropriate DSM III R rather than the old DSM III has been cited or quoted (and the quotations are extensive).

In the chapter on impotence, some new "forms" of impotence, especially in the area of psychic impotence, are noted (my thanks to Father Richard Bauhoff for sharing with me his insights in this area). In the chapter on Lack of Due Competence, General Remarks I have clarified and, to an extent, changed my position on perpetuity and this has involved corresponding changes in regard to each of the specific chapters under that heading. The chapter on Defective Convalidation has been completely rewritten. And finally, except for "The Value of Presumptions," all the old appendices have been dropped (they were, in one way or another, incorporated into *Procedures*) and three new ones have been added.

There are many other additions and changes as well, but these, it seems, are the more significant ones.

Two final points: first the omission of a chapter on error of quality (C. 1097 §2) is intentional, as explained on page 116; and secondly, references to *Decisions, Procedures* and previous editions of *Annulments* are made simpy by D, P and A respectively.

Lawrence G. Wrenn

Hartford, Connecticut
October 4, 1988
Feast of St. Francis of Assisi

INTRODUCTION

NOTES ON CANONICAL JURISPRUDENCE

A. The Meaning Of Canonical Jurisprudence

1. Definition

   Canonical jurisprudence is the science and art of utilizing, interpreting, and supplying for the codified law by rescript and by judicial sentence.

2. Explanation of Definition

   a. *Utilizing* means the fitting of a clear law to a corresponding situation. An example might be the fitting of C. 1101 § 2 (which says, among other things, that excluding perpetuity by a "positive act of the will" vitiates marriage) to a case where one party positively intended to obtain a divorce if the marriage proved unhappy.

   b. *Interpreting* means explaining the sense of a law that is obscure, at least as it applies to a particular situation. An example would be extending C. 1101 § 2 to a case where one party believed so firmly in the dissolubility of marriage (error pervicax seu radicatus) that the error itself would inevitably be applied to a particular marriage and would therefore, in practice, be tantamount to (since it would certainly lead to) a positive exclusion of perpetuity.

   c. *Supplying* means creating a new norm where there is no express law. One example would be declaring a marriage null on the grounds that an essential property of marriage was excluded not by a positive act of the will but by an inadequate commitment. Another, much more successful example of supplementation, was the pre-Code development of the notion of lack of due competence which finally culminated in C. 1095, 3^0.

3. Significance of Definition

   The general significance of defining jurisprudence as an art is that it gives to the local judge a degree of autonomy. One that must be used responsibly, of course, but still, it lifts the judge above the level of a mere enforcement officer. The local judge is not one who merely applies the judicial principles determined by higher courts. More specifically:

   a. *Utilization* - Occasionally a perfectly clear law goes unutilized. The old C. 1134 (like the present C. 1157), for example, said that, in a convalidation ceremony, the parties must personally recognize the former ceremony as invalid. It is only recently, however, that this law has been widely utilized in the United States to declare invalid

1

ceremonies where a party viewed the convalidation as a mere blessing of an already valid marriage.

b. *Interpretation* - C. 16 points out that there are two interpreters of law: the legislator and the judge. When the legislator officially interprets a law, the interpretation has the same force as the law itself but when a judge interprets a law it does not have the force of law and affects only the parties involved in the case.

This is true per se. But per accidens, namely by the force of consuetudinary law, the interpretations of judges can become the law. If, in other words, all judges hand down like decisions over a period of thirty years, the interpretation is then tantamount to law (C. 26). Or, to put it another way, the original law, at that point, may no longer be regarded as obscure. Later judges should view it as a clear law to be utilized according to the generally accepted sense.

The Code (C. 17) recommends that, in interpreting a law, the judge should look to various sources: other similar laws, the purpose of the law, the circumstances, and the mind of the legislator. Interestingly, it does not recommend that he look to the interpretations of other judges, even rotal judges.

c. *Supplementation* - When there is a lacuna or deficiency in the law, the Code views this situation as somewhat more urgent and delicate than it does an unclear law that needs interpreting. To fill the lacuna C. 19 suggests four sources, one of which is "the jurisprudence and practice of the Roman Curia," which, for the most part, means rotal jurisprudence.

Rotal supplementation does not, of course, have legal force but only suppletive force. A Rotal supplementation, in other words, is a priori recommended as safe. It has something more than its own intrinsic wisdom (which is all a supplementation by any other court has) to recommend it. This "Goodchurchkeeping Seal of Approval" awards a certain dignity to the Rota. On the other hand, it should not rob the local court of its independence, or make it excessively reliant on the Rota, because ultimately the real value of jurisprudence is not extrinsic (based on authority) but intrinsic (based on the merits of the legal argument).

There would seem to be only one occasion where a Rotal supplementation would be binding on a lower court and that would be when the following three conditions are verified: 1) some suppletory norm is required, 2) the lower court, using the other sources mentioned in C. 19, cannot supply its own norm and 3) the lower court cannot disprove the legitimacy of the Rota's norm.

B. The Development Of Canonical Jurisprudence

1. Like any other science, jurisprudence is dynamic and always evolving. It does this in the following ways:

   a. *Utilization,* i.e. by newly utilizing forgotten laws. The 1917 Code, for example, required, as noted above, that both parties in a convalidation 1) recognize the invalidity of the first ceremony and therefore 2) give a new exchange of consent at the time of the validation. It was not, however, until after the decision of January 2, 1969 coram Rogers that Tribunals began to investigate the possibility of declaring marriages null on this basis.

   b. *Application,* i.e. by finding new applications (because the cultural conditions or circumstances change) for old laws. It has, for example, always been understood that an intention against perpetuity is invalidating. In recent years, however, the prevalence of the divorce mentality in our culture has made for much broader applications of that source of nullity than was true in the past.

   c. *Restoration,* i.e. by restoring old laws or principles that were not included in the Code. Both Peter Lombard and Thomas Aquinas, for example, held that when a couple consents to marry, their consent is not simply to sexual intercourse but to a broader interpersonal relationship as well. That principle was not incorporated in the 1917 Code but was, through jurisprudence, restored, and was finally incorporated in the 1983 Code.

   d. *Expansion,* i.e. by expanding the sense of a principle to include new situations. Substantial error, for example, has always been regarded as a ground of nullity. In the 1917 Code, however, and for many years thereafter, error was, in practice, considered to be invalidating only when it involved mistaking one physical person for another (e.g. Leah for Rachel). In recent decades, however, that notion was expanded to include the situation where a person enters marriage deceived by fraud about some important quality.

   e. *Contraction,* i.e. by giving a more restrictive interpretation to a law than had been previously given. Prior to 1977, for example, the marriage of a doubly vasectomized man was considered null by Church courts. After the decree of May 13, 1977, however, vasectomy was, in itself, no longer considered a source of marital nullity.

2. In recent years there have been two major influences on the development of jurisprudence. The first major influence was the Second Vatican Council, with its insight into the nature of the marriage covenant. The second was the mental health sciences, with their insights into psychic disorders and the effect of these disorders on the consensual and functional capabilities of people.

3

C. The Roman Rota

1. Title

The Roman Wheel, as this great Tribunal is called, is most likely referred to as "The Wheel" either because the judges originally sat in a circle, or because there was a circle on the chamber floor at Avignon where the title is first known to have been used (circa A.D. 1350), or because the cases under consideration were moved from judge to judge on a bookstand which was on wheels. At any rate, the Rota has not only retained the name but still uses the wheel as its logo.

2. History of the Rota and Its Auditors

The Rota dates back at least to the twelfth century, though in those days the auditors, who were the Pope's chaplains, were only auditors and not judges as they are today. In the early days, in other words, the Pope's chaplains sat in an auditorium and took or audited the testimony, but only the Pope judged the cases. Today a judge on the Rota is still referred to as an auditor, but he has, of course, full judicial power.

There are twenty such auditors today. Ten are from Italy; two are from the United States and there is one from each of the following countries: Brazil, Czechoslovakia, France, Germany, Ireland, Lebanon, Poland and Spain. They are listed in the *Annuario Pontificio* according to the date of their Rotal appointment and are, in theory, assigned cases according to that listing in turns or boards of three in such a way that what might be called the first case would be heard by the three senior auditors, the next case by the second, third and fourth auditors and so on. The senior man on each turn is the Ponens or Commissioner and the sentence is frequently cited by referring to him: one might, for example, refer to a case "before Wynen" or "coram Wynen."

In 1870 when the Italian army invaded Rome the doors of the Rota were closed and they did not open again until 1908 when the Rota was revived by Pope Pius X. This marks, as it were, the beginning of the Rota's modern era.

3. Published Sentences

a. Enumeration of the Volumes

Volume I of the Rota's published sentences contains the decisions of 1909, the year following the Rota's revival. Each volume number, therefore, always lags eight numbers behind the year, so that volume 50, for example, contains the decisions for the year 1958.

b. The Work Load

A general idea of the Rota's case load over the years can be seen in the

the following table:

Year	Cases Decided
1912	42
1922	40
1932	59
1942	81
1952	188
1962	131
1972	306
1982	182

c. Citing a Rotal Decision

The year 1954 introduced a new way of citing rotal decisions. Up to 1953 the decisions were numbered in Roman numerals both in the Table of Contents and in the text, and a citation would include the volume number, the decision number and the page number. In 1954, however, the decision number was dropped altogether from the text, and received an Arabic number in the Table of Contents. Since it was dropped from the text it has also commonly been dropped from the citation and a sentence formerly referred to as XX, XXXV, 323 is now generally cited simply as 20, 323. In formal citations, the numbers are preceded by S.R.R.D. (Sacrae Romanae Rotae Decisiones).

d. Indexing the Volumes

The indexing of rotal decisions also saw a change in 1954. Up until 1953 each volume of decisions contained two indexes. One was a long summary (it comprised 32 pages in the 1953 Volume and 66 pages in the 1950 Volume) of all the jurisprudence contained in the volume. This was called the *Index Rerum Notabilium* and amounted to a cursillo in jurisprudence. The other index was called the *Tabula Rerum* and was a brief listing (a page and a half in 1953) of all the sentences under each principal ground for nullity.

In 1954 and 1955 the Index was discontinued and only the Tabula retained.

In 1956 a new system was introduced, namely the *Index Rerum Analyticus* which was a kind of expanded tabula listing both the generic and specific grounds with references to the pertinent sentences. Under the heading of amentia, for example, the 1956 index (which was four pages long) listed the following subheadings: homosexuality, lucid interval, paralysis, phrenasthenia and moral imbecility, psychasthenia, manic depressive psychosis and schizophrenia.

5

In 1957 the *Index Rerum Analyticus* was retained but was lengthened to twenty pages in order to include a precis of the specific point of law under each subheading.

This is by far the best indexing system to date. Under the old system neither the index nor the tabula was of much use, the first being too long and the second too short. The analytical index of 1956 was a definite improvement and the 1957 edition offers us finally a highly functional system of indexing. In 1962 the word "Analyticus" was dropped, but otherwise the Index has, for the most part, remained unchanged since 1957.

4. Value

The Rota is certainly the chief source of canonical jurisprudence for all other courts. It has set the tone and established virtually singlehandedly the traditional jurisprudence to which all other Tribunals turn. And it has done so with masterly finesse and thoroughness, especially in the area of utilizing the law.

In the areas of interpreting and supplying, rotal auditors, as might be expected, often take divergent positions on a given question. Generally, however, they are thorough, excellent theoreticians, and, especially considering their distance from the people involved, remarkably empathetic. Local judges, on the other hand, though sometimes inferior as theoreticians, nevertheless have their own pragmatic strengths. Their understanding of the capacities of people, an understanding gained from broad, clinical experience, seems especially acute and real; and they have a high awareness and sensitivity to local conditions and their importance.

The challenge, at any rate, is the same for all judges, both rotal and local. They must know their own culture and their own times. They must be able to perceive, and to weigh, and to create suitable, enlightened norms by which justice can be rendered. They must avoid the extremes of being insensitive on the one hand, and pandering on the other; of being too theoretical on the one hand, and too intuitive on the other. They must be neither too legalistic nor too romantic, neither too demanding nor too excusing. They must, above all, show forth the ability of the Church to treat people as individual persons of the community and not just as cases or stereotypes. Only in this way can jurisprudence continue to be the "ars boni et aequi" for each succeeding generation.

6

MALE IMPOTENCE

A. The Pertinent Canon

C. 1084 §1 - Antecedent and perpetual impotence to have intercourse, whether on the part of the man or of the woman, which is either absolute or relative, of its very nature invalidates marriage.

§2 - If the impediment of impotence is doubtful, either by reason of a doubt of law or a doubt of fact, a marriage is neither to be impeded nor is it to be declared null as long as the doubt exists.

§3 - Sterility neither prohibits nor invalidates marriage, with due regard for the prescription of canon 1098.

B. Impotence As An Impediment

1. Impotence is regarded in the law as a diriment impediment. C. 1084 is found in Chapter III - "On Specific Diriment Impediments." A diriment impediment, says C. 1073, "renders a person incapable (inhabilem) of validly contracting marriage."

2. A diriment impediment, understood in the strict sense, is a "lex inhabilitans," a law which disables a person, who is per se capable, from entering a marriage. The diriment impediments of disparity of cult, sacred orders, public vow, etc., as found in canons 1086-1094, are all diriment impediments taken in this strict sense.

3. Some canonists have noted that impotence is not really an impediment in the strict sense, because the impotent person is not per se capable of marriage. The impotent person is incapable of assuming the essential obligations of marriage and is therefore incapable of placing the object of marital consent and is therefore incapable of marriage. See Navarrete, Urbano, "Incapacitas Assumendi Onera Uti Caput Autonomum Nullitatis Matrimonii" in *Periodica*, 1972, 1, p. 78-80.

4. Impotence, therefore, is a diriment impediment in a somewhat wider sense. The fact is, however, that, in canon law, impotence is regarded not as a defect of consent but as a diriment impediment.

5. Incompetence (lack of due competence) has much in common with impotence, not just phonetically but really. Taxonomically, however, they differ. Impotence is classified as an impediment; incompetence as a defect of consent. See the chapter entitled "Lack of Due Competence - General Remarks."

C. Definition Of The Impediment Of Impotence

1. The diriment impediment of impotence may be defined as the antecedent and perpetual incapacity of a man or woman to have physical intercourse.

2. Three notions in this definition merit comment: a) the meaning of intercourse, b) that the impediment be antecedent, and c) that it be perpetual.

   a. *Intercourse*

   For the man to be capable of intercourse, three elements must be present: erection, penetration, and ejaculation during intercourse.

   Whether the man, to be potent, must be capable of ejaculating *within the vagina* is somewhat questionable (*Communicationes,* 1974, 2, pp. 177-196 and 1975, 1, pp. 58-60). Therefore, in view of C. 1084 §2, a man who can ejaculate during intercourse, but not within the vagina, would be regarded not as impotent but only as sterile. This would apply particularly to the man afflicted with either hypospadias (where the opening of the urethra is on the undersurface of the penis) or epispadias (on the dorsal surface) where these conditions might prevent depositing semen within the vagina. The man, however, who is incapable of any real, i.e. antegrade ejaculation must be regarded as not just sterile but impotent (see the Dublin decision in *Monitor Ecclesiasticus,* 1987, IV, pp. 485-495).

   b. *Antecedent*

   Although impotence, to be invalidating, must be antecedent (on the obvious grounds that no supervenient factor can affect validity), it is not required that the impotence should have manifested itself beforehand. It is not required that the impotence be actual or dynamic at the time of marriage, but only that it be virtual or causal. It is necessary and it suffices that the proximate disposition to impotence and the proximate causes of its onset be present at the time of marriage. This could be verified, for example, in the case of a homosexual but not in the case of a heterosexual who found himself impotent after marriage because he found his wife's obnoxious personal habits repulsive.

   c. *Perpetual*

   Impotence is considered to be perpetual when, at least relative to the marriage in question, it is incurable or when it is curable only by 1) a miracle, 2) illicit means, 3) probable danger to one's life, 4) serious harm to one's health or 5) doubtfully successful means. Or, to put it another way, impotence is perpetual when, at least relative to the marriage in question, it is irremediable except by extraordinary means.

It should be noted, however, that to be invalidating, the impotence must be perpetual at the time of the marriage and not simply become so later. It is possible, in other words, that a man was de facto impotent at the time of marriage, but that he was not suffering from the impediment of impotence at that time, since it was then curable. Perhaps the impotence later became incurable but that does not affect validity. Nevertheless, if the experts can testify as regards *absolute* impotence (where the man is impotent in respect to women in general) that the very form of impotence from which the man suffers is incurable, or was at the time of marriage; and as regards *relative* impotence (where the man is impotent in respect to a particular woman) that he could at no stage of the marriage have been cured in respect to his wife, then the marriage would be considered null.

D. Causes Of Impotence

Impotence can be either organic or functional. *Organic* impotence arises from the fact that the sexual organs themselves are physically, anatomically or organically defective whereas in *functional* impotence the organs themselves are organically perfect but for one reason or another (either neurophysiological or psychical) they function imperfectly.

E. Forms Of Impotence

1. Organic

    a. Absence of the penis
    b. Abnormal size or shape of the penis preventing vaginal intromission
    c. Retrograde ejaculation (could also be Functional)

2. Functional
    a. Physical

    Paraplegia (a paralysis of the lower extremities of the body resulting from disease or injury to the central nervous system) and other similar infirmities when this does in fact render intercourse impossible. Brenkle notes that in fact about 70% of paraplegics are capable of erection but only about 10% of them are capable of ejaculation. (Brenkle, John, *The Impediment of Male Impotence with Special Application to Paraplegia*, Washington, D.C., CUA Press, 1963, pp. 156-157).

    b. Psychic

    1) Inability to obtain or sustain an erection (anaphrodisia).
    2) Excessive excitability resulting in premature ejaculation (aphrodisia).
    3) Ejaculatory Incompetence, also called Inhibited Male Orgasm, which is the opposite of premature ejaculation, namely

9

the inability of the man to ejaculate during intercourse. See *Human Sexual Inadequacy* Masters and Johnson, pp. 116-136 and DSM III R, p. 295.

4) Dyspareunia
   a) The Syndrome

   Although the term dyspareunia, that is, painful intercourse, has traditionally referred to coital distress in women, it can, in fact, also refer to men (see DSM III R, p. 295 and Masters and Johnson, *Human Sexual Inadequacy* pp. 288-294).

   b) The Juridic Principle

   The juridic principle was stated in a decision coram Heard of December 30, 1949 (*Ephemerides Iuris Canonici,* VII (1951) 3-4, p. 363). Speaking of intercourse that involved intolerable pain for the woman, Heard wrote "Such an inhuman way of acting, even if it resulted in the phsyical consummation of the marriage, would not rule out the impediment of impotence; for just as no one is legally bound to undergo a surgical operation which would endanger one's life, so no one is legally bound to have intercourse which would necessarily involve intolerable pain."

   It should be noted too that in order for a marriage to be regarded as consummated the couple must have had intercourse "in a human manner" (C. 1061 §1), which would certainly mean that it did not cause either party intolerable pain.

   Some would perhaps argue that Heard went too far in admitting that physical consummation could coexist with impotence (his decision was not included in the 1949 volume of Rotal decisions) but there would presumably be general agreement among jurists that where intolerable pain does, in fact, render complete intercourse (erection, penetration and ejaculation) impossible, then the condition would, if proved antecedent and perpetual, constitute the impediment of impotence.

F.   Proof Of Impotence

In regard to organic impotence and functional-physical impotence, the proofs will consist almost entirely of medical reports. In regard to functional-psychic impotence, the Court must depend on the declarations of the parties, affidavits and testimony of witnesses, etc. (for the canons on this type of proof, see the chapters on simulation). When impotence results from a psychological cause, however, it is usually symptomatic of a more pervasive syndrome and can often be viewed more easily and more accurately under the heading of lack of due competence.

G. The Decree Of May 13, 1977

1. The jurisprudence outlined above reflects the tenor of the Decree of the Congregation of the Doctrine of the Faith, approved by the Pope on May 13, 1977. See D2, pp. 1-2.

2. Prior to that decree jurisprudence recognized more forms of impotence (see Section E) than it does at present. Men, for example, who had been doubly vasectomized, even though they were entirely capable of erection, penetration and ejaculation, were regarded as impotent before the decree.

3. *Some* canonists are of the opinion that the decree was not retroactive. This is a well founded opinion based on seeing the decree as an authentic interpretation of what had been a dubious law. C. 16 §2 (C. 17 §2 in the 1917 Code) specifically states that such a decree is *not* retroactive. *Other* canonists, however, are of the opinion that the decree simply declared the true meaning of impotence, which meaning had always been intrinsically certain (in se certa) even though not properly understood by everyone. C. 16 §2 states that such a decree *is* retroactive. This position is also well founded.

4. Because of these two well founded but conflicting opinions we are left with a doubt of law regarding the retroactivity of the decree. According to the first opinion there were more forms of impotence before the effective date of the decree than there were afterwards. This, however, is only a probable opinion. Therefore the "extra forms" of impotence, e.g. vasectomy, that were accepted by many prior to the decree were, in fact, only doubtful impediments. According to C. 1084 §2, however, a doubtful impediment is no impediment. In practice, therefore, the presently accepted jurisprudence (as outlined in Sections A-E above) may be regarded as the proper jurisprudence to apply to all marriages, of whatever date, that come to the attention of a tribunal.

11

A. The Pertinent Canon

C. 1084 §1 - Antecedent and perpetual impotence to have intercourse, whether on the part of the man or of the woman, which is either absolute or relative, of its very nature invalidates marriage.

§2 - If the impediment of impotence is doubtful, either by reason of a doubt of law or a doubt of fact, a marriage is neither to be impeded nor is it to be declared null as long as the doubt exists.

§3 - Sterility neither prohibits nor invalidates marriage, with due regard for the prescription of canon 1098.

B. Impotence As An Impediment

1. Impotence is regarded in the law as a diriment impediment. C. 1084 is found in Chapter III - "On Specific Diriment Impediments." A diriment impediment, says C. 1073, "renders a person incapable (inhabilem) of contracting marriage validly."

2. A diriment impediment, understood in the strict sense, is a "lex inhabilitans," a law which disables a person, who is per se capable, from entering a marriage. The diriment impediments of disparity of cult, sacred orders, public vow, etc., as found in canons 1086-1094, are all diriment impediments taken in this strict sense.

3. Some canonists have noted that impotence is not really an impediment in the strict sense, because the impotent person is not per se capable of marriage. The impotent person is incapable of assuming the essential obligations of marriage and is therefore incapable of placing the object of marital consent and is therefore incapable of marriage. See Navarrete, Urbano, "Incapacitas Assumendi Onera Uti Caput Autonomum Nullitatis Matrimonii" in *Periodica*, 1972, 1, p. 78-80.

4. Impotence, therefore, is a diriment impediment in a somewhat wider sense. The fact is, however, that, in canon law, impotence is regarded not as a defect of consent but as a diriment impediment.

5. Incompetence (lack of due competence) has much in common with impotence, not just phonetically but really. Taxonomically, however, they differ. Impotence is classified as an impediment; incompetence as a defect of consent. See the chapter entitled "Lack of Due Competence - General Remarks."

C. Definition Of The Impediment Of Impotence

1. The diriment impediment of impotence may be defined as the antecedent and perpetual incapacity of a man or woman to have physical intercourse.

2. Three notions in this definition merit comment: a) the meaning of intercourse, b) that the impediment be antecedent, and c) that it be perpetual.

a. *Intercourse*

For a woman to be organically capable of intercourse, she must have a vagina that is capable of receiving the erect male member. The vagina need not be natural. Even an artificial vagina would suffice. See the decision coram Raad of October 16, 1980 in D2, pp. 5-8.

b. *Antecedent*

Although impotence, to be invalidating, must be antecedent (on the obvious grounds that no supervenient factor can affect validity) it is not required that the impotence should have manifested itself beforehand. It is not required that the impotence be actual or dynamic at the time of marriage, but only that it be virtual or causal. It is necessary and it suffices that the proximate disposition to impotence and the proximate causes of its onset be present at the time of the marriage. This would be verified, for example, when the woman finds after marriage that she suffers from vaginismus due to a previous traumatic experience.

c. *Perpetual*

Impotence is considered to be perpetual when, at least relative to the marriage in question, it is incurable or when it is curable only by 1) a miracle, 2) illicit means, 3) probable danger to one's life, 4) serious harm to one's health or 5) doubtfully successful means. Or, to put it another way, impotence is perpetual when, at least relative to the marriage in question, it is irremediable except by extraordinary means.

It should be noted, however, that, to be invalidating, the impotence must be perpetual at the time of the marriage, and not simply become so later. It is possible, in other words, that a woman was de facto impotent at the time of marriage, but that she was not suffering from the impediment of impotence at that time, since it was then curable. Perhaps the impotence later became incurable but that does not affect validity. Nevertheless, if the experts can testify as regards *absolute* impotence (where the woman is impotent in respect to men in general) that the very form of impotence from which the woman suffers is incurable, or was at the time of marriage; and as regards *relative* impotence (where the woman is impotent in respect to a particular man) that she could at no stage of the marriage have been cured in respect to her husband, then the marriage would be considered null.

D. Causes Of Impotence

Impotence can be either organic or functional. *Organic* impotence arises from the fact that the sexual organs themselves are physically, anatomically or organically defective whereas in *functional* impotence the organs themselves are organically perfect but for one reason or another (either physical or psychical) they function imperfectly.

E. Forms Of Impotence

1. Organic

   A woman is considered organically impotent when she lacks a vagina (whether natural or artificial) of sufficient width and length to receive the erect male member.

2. Functional

   A woman is considered functionally impotent when intercourse is either impossible due to vaginismus or intolerably painful due to Female Sexual Arousal Disorder or Dyspareunia.

   a. *Vaginismus*

      In a decision of October 9, 1964 (56, 682) Sabattani discussed the legal aspects of vaginismus. It may be summarized as follows:

      1) *Definition* - Vaginismus may be defined as the painful spasm of all the muscles surrounding and supporting the vagina which happens when intercourse is attempted or even when the area is merely touched and which renders intercourse impossible.

      2) *Division*

         a) Schema

Symptomatic	Neurasthenic	Defensive	Conversion Hysteria
Idiopathic	Psychogenic		Anxiety Hysteria
Mixed	Psychotic	Repulsive	

14

b)   Discussion

Vaginismus is called *symptomatic* when there are present pathologic, inflammatory lesions of the urogenital structures due either to immoderate or violent attempts at intercourse or to hypersensitivity or to some injury or infection. It is called *idiopathic* when the vaginal contraction is caused by neurological or psychological factors only, without there being present any anatomic factors. It is called *mixed* when both factors are present.

Idiopathic vaginismus is called *neurasthenic* when it is of a temporary, passing nature. It is called *psychogenic* when it is a more permanent, constitutional problem. It is called *psychotic* when it is existing concomitantly with and probably as a symptom of an underlying psychosis.

Psychogenic vaginismus is called *defensive* whenever it is merely a subconscious defense mechanism against pain or against a hated husband. It is called *repulsive* when it creates in the woman an abhorrence for sexual relations.

Defensive vaginismus is manifested in an *anxiety hysteria* where it results from a real or suspected violent or inhuman approach by the man and by a *conversion hysteria* where it results not from a faulty approach but from a pathological fear of pain resulting from the insertion of the penis. In this case, the woman, in effect, "converts" this fear of pain into a real pain, namely that resulting from the vaginal contraction.

3)   *Presumptions Regarding Antecedence and Perpetuity*

a)   *Symptomatic* vaginismus is not presumed either to be antecedent or supervenient. In a given case, however, it could be proved to have been antecedent. It is only considered perpetual when its organic basis can be proved incurable. Otherwise it is presumed to be temporary.

b)   *Neurasthenic* vaginismus is not presumed either to be antecedent or perpetual.

c)   The *conversion hysteria* type of defensive vaginismus is presumed to be antecedent if it is present on the first attempt at intercourse. As for perpetuity, there is no presumption favoring perpetuity because it can ordinarily be cured by psychotherapy.

d)   The *anxiety hysteria* type follows the same general presumptions but it should be noted here that in this case the woman could well be relatively impotent, that is, she could be impotent towards the man who originally approached her in an insensitive way.

15

e) *Repulsive* vaginismus is presumed antecedent if it is present on the first attempt at intercourse. It is also presumed perpetual - because it is extremely serious and because therapy is not usually successful. There is always the possibility of an operation of course. But if this is just a hymenal operation like a hymenectomy, it will not really cure the vaginismus and if it is an operation on the nervous system, then it would have to be considered an extraordinary means.

f) *Psychotic* vaginismus is presumed antecedent if present on the first attempt at intercourse and is also presumed perpetual.

g) *Mixed* vaginismus depends for its ruling presumptions on the prevailing aspect, either symptomatic or idiopathic.

4) *Criteria For Judging Circumstantial Evidence*

The following criteria might be helpful in confirming the presence of an invalidating vaginismus. If most of these are present in a given case without being contravened by other evidence the marriage should certainly be declared null.

a) Objective Criteria - if the medical examination (preferably extra-judicial tolerated by the woman for the sake of a cure rather than at the request of the court) reveals immediate, obvious and intense spasms and if, because of the woman's abhorrence and sensitivity, the examination is finally conducted only with great difficulty.

b) Subjective Criteria - if the woman, although truly in love with her husband, becomes extremely agitated and even hysterical on the wedding night and if she honestly but vainly tries to submit to intercourse in order to save the marriage.

c) Psycho-Physical Criteria - if the vaginismus is accompanied by serious hypoplasia (inadequate evolution of the female organs), if the woman has a neuropsychopathic constitution, if she cries out in pain and even becomes convulsive during attempts at intercourse and if she speaks of or actually attempts suicide.

d) Temporal Criteria - if the couple remained in love and stayed together for a long time and if the woman was diagnosed as suffering from severe vaginismus on many occasions all through her life, even after the separation, with no cure ever effected.

b. *Female Sexual Arousal Disorder and Dyspareunia*

1) The Syndromes

DSM III R (pp. 294-295) briefly describes these two disorders. The former involves a persistent or recurrent partial or complete failure

16

to attain or maintain the lubrication-swelling response of sexual excitement until completion of the sexual activity. The latter involves recurrent or persistent pain before, during or after sexual intercourse. Both disorders can conceivably involve intolerable pain for the woman whenever intercourse is engaged in.

2) The Juridic Principle

The juridic principle was stated in a decision coram Heard of December 30, 1949 (*Ephemerides Iuris Canonici*, VII (1951) 3-4, p. 363). Speaking of intercourse that involved intolerable pain for the woman, Heard wrote "Such an inhuman way of acting, even if it resulted in the physical consummation of the marriage, would not rule out the impediment of impotence; for just as no one is legally bound to undergo a surgical operation which would endanger one's life, so no one is legally bound to have intercourse which would necessarily involve intolerable pain."

It should be noted too that in order for a marriage to be regarded as consummated the couple must have had intercourse "in a human manner" (C. 1061 §1), which would certainly mean that it did not cause either party intolerable pain.

Some would perhaps argue that Heard went too far in admitting that physical consummation could coexist with impotence (his decision was not included in the 1949 volume of Rotal decisions) but there would presumably be general agreement among jurists that where intolerable pain does, in fact, render complete intercourse (erection, penetration and ejaculation) impossible, then the condition would, if proved antecedent and perpetual, constitute the impediment of impotence.

F. Proof Of Impotence

Proof of organic impotence will consist almost entirely in medical reports. Proof of functional impotence will often include the declarations of the parties, affidavits and testimony of witnesses, etc. (for the canons on this type of proof, see the chapters on simulation). It should be noted, too, that functional impotence often involves deep-seated psychological problems on the part of the woman, in which case a report from a psychiatric expert is useful. See the Tern-Kapaun case in D1, pp. 5-7. And finally it should be noted that when the perpetuity of the disorder cannot be proved, as is often the case, especially with Female Sexual Arousal Disorder and Dyspareunia, then the case can often, in practice, be handled more easily on the grounds of incompetence (C. 1095, 3°) than on the grounds of impotence (C. 1084).

G. The Decree Of May 13, 1977

1. The jurisprudence outlined above reflects the tenor, as applied to the woman, of the Decree of the Congregation of the Doctrine of the Faith, approved by the Pope on May 13, 1977. See D2, pp. 1-2.

2. Prior to that decree jurisprudence recognized more forms of impotence (see Section E) than it does at present. Women, for example, who had an artificial vagina at the time of marriage, even though it was quite capable of receiving the erect male member, were regarded as impotent before the decree.

3. *Some* canonists are of the opinion that the decree was not retroactive. This is a well founded opinion based on seeing the decree as an authentic interpretation of what had been a dubious law. C. 16 §2 (C. 17 §2 in the 1917 Code) specifically states that such a decree is *not* retroactive. *Other* canonists, however, are of the opinion that the decree simply declared the true meaning of impotence, which meaning had always been intrinsically certain (in se certa) even though not properly understood by everyone. C. 16 §2 states that such a decree *is* retroactive. This position is also well founded.

4. Because of these two well founded but conflicting opinions we are left with a doubt of law regarding the retroactivity of the decree. According to the first opinion there were more forms of impotence before the effective date of the decree than there were afterwards. This, however, is only a probable opinion. Therefore the "extra forms" of impotence, e.g. absence of a natural vagina, that were accepted by many prior to the decree were, in fact, only doubtful impediments. According to C. 1084 §2, however, a doubtful impediment is no impediment. In practice, therefore, the presently accepted jurisprudence (as outlined in Sections A-E above) may be regarded as the proper jurisprudence to apply to all marriages, of whatever date, that come to the attention of a tribunal.

A. The Pertinent Canon

C. 1095   - They are incapable of contracting marriage
    1° - who lack the sufficient use of reason

B. The Context Of The Canon

This 1° of C. 1095 (on lack of due *reason*) is perhaps best understood in conjunction with 2° (on lack of due *discretion*) and 3° (on lack of due *competence*). These read as follows:

C. 1095   - They are incapable of contracting marriage
    2° - who suffer from grave lack of discretion of judgment concerning essential matrimonial rights and duties which are to be mutually given and accepted;
    3° - who are not strong enough to assume the essential obligations of matrimony due to causes of a psychic nature.

C. The Meaning Of Lack Of Due Reason

1. When C. 1095 1° speaks of a lack of *sufficient* use of reason, it is not, of course, referring to a *simple* use of reason. It is not suggesting, in other words, that once one has attained the use of reason and can place a human act, he or she is capable of marriage. It is, rather, saying that, in order to be capable of marriage, one must have arrived at a degree of reasoning ability sufficient to understand that, in marrying, "a man and a woman give and receive each other by an irrevocable covenant to constitute . . . a partnership of the spouses' entire life, a partnership ordered, by its nature, to the good of the spouses and the procreation and education of children" (CC. 1057 §2 and 1055 §2).

2. When compared with 2° of this canon, however, 1° seems to be referring to a fairly primitive, conceptual understanding of the nature of marriage, whereas 2° is referring to a more mature, sophisticated, evaluative judgment regarding the rights and duties to be handed over.

In a sense, therefore, 1° is superfluous. The two numbers together are rather like saying: 1) one may not join the army before the age of 10, 2) one may not join the army before the age of 18.

Nevertheless, this number one of C. 1095 does have the advantage of reflecting the historical background of the canon and may even be put to use in cases where sufficient use of reason is, in fact, lacking. See D2 pp. 10-15 and 37-39.

D. The Cause Of Lack Of Due Reason

In order for an adult to be deprived of something as basic as the sufficient use of reason, he or she would have to be affected by a fairly serious condition. Traditionally such conditions have been divided into transitory and habitual (see 58, 180 and A1 and A2, pp. 20 and 21 respectively). The 1980 draft of this canon retained that division by noting that lack of sufficient reason could be caused either by a disturbance (transitory) or by a disorder (habitual).

Although the Code itself has eliminated any reference to the causality of the lack of sufficient reason, the traditional distinction remains of some use in jurisprudence. Examples of an *habitual* disorder that would deprive a person of the sufficient use of reason would be schizophrenia (see D2, pp. 10-15) and profound mental retardation. Examples of a *transitory* disturbance that would produce the same effect would be alcoholic intoxication and an epileptic ictal twilight state.

E. The Result Of Lack Of Due Reason

When a person lacks due reason, the result is that that person cannot give consent (nil volitum nisi praecognitum). Ultimately it is this inability to give consent that invalidates the marriage, as is clear from the fact that this canon is located in Chapter IV which is entitled "On Matrimonial Consent."

This is appropriate. It is, after all, consent that makes marriage (consensus facit nuptias). As C. 1057 §1 says, "Marriage is brought about through the consent of the parties, legitimately manifested between persons who are capable according to law of giving consent; no human power can replace this consent."

F. Proof Of Lack Of Due Reason

1. *Parties, Affiants and Witnesses*

In cases involving an alleged lack of due reason every effort should be made to obtain testimony from the respondent (usually the party whose lack of due reason is alleged). Sometimes the petitioner has lost touch with the respondent and cannot provide an address but usually, with a little effort, the respondent can be located.

The declarations of the parties and the affidavits and testimony of others are extremely important in these cases since they provide the data on which a judgment can be made. For the canons pertaining to the evaluation of this evidence, see one of the four chapters on simulation (total simulation, intentions against children, fidelity and perpetuity) in the section on proof.

2. *Experts*

    a.   *The Law*

C. 1680 reads as follows: In cases of impotence or of defect of consent due to a mental illness the judge is to use the services of one or more experts unless it is obvious from the circumstances that this would be useless; in other cases the prescription of C. 1574 is to be observed.

C. 1574 says: The services of experts must be used whenever their examination and opinion, based on the laws of art or science, are required in order to establish some fact or to clarify the true nature of some thing by reason of a prescription of the law or a judge.

    b.   *An Observation*

It is clear, first of all, as noted under E, that this ground does involve a "defect of consent." Taken together, therefore, the two canons seem to be saying that when the cause of the lack of due reason is some *habitual* disorder, the services of an expert are (unless they would be clearly superfluous) required, whereas, when the cause is of a *transitory* nature, their use is at the discretion of the judge.

    c.   *The Probative Force*

C. 1579 §1 says that the judge is to weigh attentively not only the conclusions of the experts but also the other circumstances of the case. This is a reminder that the judge is the *peritus peritorum* and that, besides the report of the expert, the judge must also be concerned with such questions as whether the data on which the conclusions of the expert are based are truly proved by the evidence. It is in this sense that the *dicta peritorum cribranda sunt,* i.e., that the report of the expert should be "sifted." At the same time, however, *peritis in arte credendum est* and, as Parisella noted, "When it comes to evaluating the weight and importance of the expert's report, the Rota has many times (see the decisions of 10/21/59 coram Lamas, of 8/5/54 coram Pinna, of 11/6/56 coram Mattioli, of 2/26/52 and 4/6/54 coram Felici) taught that it is wrong for the judge to depart from the conclusions of the experts except for very weighty contrary arguments." (60, 564-565).

LACK OF DUE DISCRETION

GENERAL REMARKS

A. The Pertinent Canon

C. 1095   - They are incapable of contracting marriage
> 2° - who suffer from grave lack of discretion of judgment concerning essential matrimonial rights and duties which are to be mutually given and accepted.

B. The Context Of The Canon

This 2° of C. 1095 (on lack of due *discretion*) is perhaps best understood in conjunction with 1° (on lack of due *reason*) and 3° (on lack of due *competence*). These read as follows:

C. 1095   - They are incapable of contracting marriage
> 1° - who lack the sufficient use of reason
> 3° - who are not strong enough to assume the essential obligations of matrimony due to causes of a psychic nature.

C. The Meaning Of Discretion

To some readers the word "discretion," and a fortiori the term "discretion of judgment," sound as though they refer exclusively to the intellect. This, however, is not the case. The truth is that, in jurisprudence, the term refers to both the intellect and the will. What is required for discretion is that 1) the intellect make a mature evaluation and 2) the will make a free choice.

The inclusion of both intellect and will under the umbrella of discretion was clearly the mind of the legislator in drafting C. 1095 2°. The present wording of the canon is, except for the insertion of the word "essential," exactly the same as in the 1980 draft of the Code (the number of the canon was then 1048 2°). In preparation for the October 1981 meeting of the Commissioners, however, one of the Commissioners suggested that the canon be changed to read, "They are incapable of contracting marriage who labor under a severe and abnormal defect of judgmental discretion to such an extent that they are unable to understand even the necessary elements of marriage." The Secretary and the Consultors, however, successfully urged that the 1980 wording be retained because, they said, "what is at issue here is not cognition or perception of the intellectual order but rather a defect of judgmental discretion" (*Relatio*, p. 254). The 1980 wording, it was noted, reflected rotal jurisprudence. And rotal jurisprudence, it might be added, has consistently understood the term discretion to include a proper functioning of both intellect and will. See, for example, D2, pp. 22-23 and 33-34.

D. The Meaning Of Due Discretion

1. Although the canon does not contain the word "due", the word *was* used by Gasparri, who pioneered the concept (see the Index of the 1932 edition of his *De Matrimonio*), and is frequently used in rotal decisions (see, for example, D2, pp. 38-39 and 60, 193; 63, 763 and 69, 233). It simply means that, in performing any action, the agent should enjoy the degree of discretion that is due or proportionate to that action. As regards the amount of discretion due marriage, Sabattani noted in his decision of February 24, 1961 (53, 118):

    > The doctrine on discretionary judgment . . . can be summed up in these words of Jullien, 'since marriage is a very serious contract which is not only future oriented but actually indissoluble, in order to enter it validly a greater degree of discretion is required than would be necessary to consent to some action which only concerned the present, as, for example, the amount of discretion required to commit a mortal sin' (27, 79).

    > Indeed, since marriage is 'a covenant filled with responsibilities in which the gift of one's whole life and being is pledged' (as Wynen said, 35, 171) then clearly 'greater freedom and deliberation is required for marriage than for other contracts' (from a decision of Grazioli 18, 111).

    > And let it be remembered that a mere *cognoscitive* faculty, which consists in the simple mental apprehension of something, is not sufficient but that there is further required a *critical* faculty, which is the ability to judge and reason and so order one's judgments that new judgments can be deduced from them (see the December 3, 1957 decision of Felici and Lamas' sentence of October 21, 1959).

    > A marriage, in short, is only valid when a person, using that critical faculty, can deliberately form judgments with his mind and freely choose actions with his will.

2. In order to consent to a valid marriage, in other words, the decision should be informed with a certain fundamental prudence. It should include, therefore, such qualities as good advice (eubulia), insight (synesis), a sense of the situation (gnome), deliberation, foresight, circumspection, appreciation, sound judgment and clear reasoning that enables the person to draw rational inferences from his insights and experiences.

    More specifically, contractants must be able to make at least a rudimentary assessment of the capacities of themselves and their spouse, and to decide freely that they wish to establish a perpetual and exclusive community of life with this person, a community that will involve a lifetime of fundamentally faithful caring and sharing.

3. The defect of discretion, as the canon notes, must be "grave" in order to be invalidating.

E. The Object Of Discretion

The canon suggests that there is both a general and a specific object of discretion.

1. General

In order to enter a valid marriage the thing one must exercise due discretion about is "the essential matrimonial rights and duties." It would be expected, therefore, that one would have some basic appreciation of the fact that marriage is a permanent, heterosexual partnership (CC 1055 §1 and 1096 §1) involving some personal sharing (C. 1135).

2. Specific

It is not, however, just matrimonial rights and duties in general that one must appreciate. It is, rather, those essential matrimonial rights which are to be mutually exchanged by these two people here and now. These rights and duties would include 1) being truthful with one's spouse, i.e. letting one's spouse know one's true identity (self revelation), 2) appreciating one's spouse as a separate, independent person (understanding), and 3) sharing a mutual affection with one's spouse (loving). If, therefore, a person radically fails to appreciate these "rights and duties," he or she lacks due discretion.

F. The Causes Of Indiscretion

Lack of due discretion is most often caused by a combination of factors, some intrinsic, some extrinsic. Among the intrinsic factors one frequently finds that the parties are quite young and/or have an identity disorder or personality disorder of at least moderate degree. Among the extrinsic factors, one often finds a premarital pregnancy or abortion, or unhappy, burdensome life in the parental home with a desire to escape, a brief courtship, belated reluctance to marry and family pressure or fear of embarrassment.

For some examples of specific causes, see the chapters immediately following. For examples of causes seen in constellation, see D2, pp. 16-45.

G. The Result Of Indiscretion

When a person lacks due discretion, the net result is that the person is deprived of the ability to consent. This is clear from the fact that this canon is found under the general rubric (Chapter IV) of Matrimonial Consent.

H. Giving Consent vs. Expressing Consent

At the time of the marriage ceremony the parties *express* their consent. Presumably they *gave* their consent, i.e. actually consented to marry some time prior to that. At the time of the ceremony, besides expressing their consent, they may but need not actually renew their consent. It suffices if their consent previously given virtually perdures and is expressed at the time of the ceremony.

In order merely to express consent already given one does not need due discretion or a critical faculty or prudence. It suffices if he can simply place a human act. It would, therefore, be very difficult to prove a marriage null simply because one of the parties was, for example, drunk at the time of the ceremony. Because at the time of the ceremony one does not have to place a *prudent* act (consenting) but simply a *human* act (expressing consent).

When, therefore, a Court investigates the matter of due discretion, the investigation does not confine itself to the moment of the ceremony but rather concerns itself with the whole period of time during which the person decided to and consented to marry.

I. Proof Of Lack Of Due Discretion

1. *Parties, Affiants and Witnesses*

In cases involving an alleged lack of due discretion every effort should be made to obtain testimony from the respondent. Sometimes the petitioner has lost touch with the respondent, and cannot provide an address, but usually, with a little effort, the respondent can be located.

The declarations of the parties and the affidavits and testimony of others are extremely important in these cases since they provide the data on which a judgment can be made. For the canons pertaining to the evaluation of this evidence, see one of the four chapters on simulation (total simulation, intentions against children, fidelity and perpetuity) in the section on proof.

2. *Experts*

a. *The Law*

C. 1680 reads as follows: In cases of impotence or defect of consent due to mental illness, the judge is to use the services of one or more experts unless it is obvious from the circumstances that this would be useless; in other cases the prescription of C. 1574 is to be observed.

C. 1574 says: The services of experts must be used whenever their examination and opinion, based on the laws of art or science, are required in order to establish some fact or to clarify the true nature of some thing by reason of a prescription of the law or a judge.

b. *An Observation*

C. 1680 notes that an expert is called when 1) there is a defect of consent and 2) there is a mentis morbus.

Lack of due discretion, as noted under G, does involve a defect of consent. The term "mentis morbus" is here translated "mental illness" or "mental disorder" because, since the first edition of the *Diagnostic and Statistical Manual* in 1952, the American Psychiatric Association has referred to all psychopathology as Mental Disorders. For practical purposes here in America, therefore, the term may be regarded as co-extensive with the disorders listed in DSM III R.

A lack of due discretion case, as noted under F, does not always involve a mental disorder. Sometimes the indiscretion is caused by predominantly extrinsic causes, frequently coupled with ordinary immaturity or prematurity. In such cases the services of an expert would be at the discretion of the judge. It is only when a true disorder is present that a perital report is required.

c. *The Probative Force*

C. 1579 §1 says that the judge is to weigh attentively not only the conclusions of the experts but also the other circumstances of the case. This is a reminder that the judge is the *peritus peritorum* and that, besides the report of the expert, the judge must also be concerned with such questions as whether the data on which the conclusions of the expert are based are truly proved by the evidence. It is in this sense that the *dicta peritorum cribranda sunt,* i.e., that the report of the expert should be "sifted." At the same time, however, *peritis in arte credendum est* and, as Parisella noted, "When it comes to evaluating the weight and importance of the expert's report, the Rota has many times (see the decisions of 10/21/59 coram Lamas, of 8/5/54 coram Pinna, of 11/6/56 coram Mattioli, of 2/26/52 and 4/6/54 coram Felici) taught that it is wrong for the judge to depart from the conclusions of the experts except for very weighty contrary arguments." (60, 564-565).

J. Use Of The Ground

It often happens that a person lacks both due discretion and due competence. In such a case a tribunal is free to select the ground on the basis of the particular circumstances. It may happen, for example, that the woman in a case is diagnosed by the expert as suffering from a Narcissistic Personality Disorder. If the woman was twenty-five years old at the time of the marriage and was married after a two year courtship, the court would be inclined to judge the case on the grounds of lack of due *competence.* If, however, the woman was sixteen and pregnant and married after a five month courtship, the court would be inclined to judge the case on the ground of lack of due *discretion.* The same is true of other disorders. Anxiety Disorders, Mood Disorders and Schizophrenia, for example, are often heard as Lack of Due Discretion rather than Lack of Due Competence cases, depending on the circumstances as well as on the jurisprudential convictions of the judge. See also D2, p. 65.

MENTAL RETARDATION

A. Description Of Mental Retardation

Mental retardation is a condition manifested by a significantly subaverage general intellectual functioning resulting in, or associated with, deficits or impairments in adaptive behavior, with onset before the age of 18.

B. Subtypes Of Mental Retardation

1. DSM IIIR lists four subtypes of mental retardation depending on intelligence quotient (IQ).

Mild	50-55 to approx. 70
Moderate	35-40 to 50-55
Severe	20-25 to 35-40
Profound	Below 20 or 25

2. These four subtypes are described by DSM III R as follows:

   a. *Mild Mental Retardation*

   Mild Mental Retardation is roughly equivalent to what used to be referred to as the educational category of "educable." This group constitutes the largest segment of those with the disorder—about 85%. People with this level of Mental Retardation typically develop social and communication skills during the preschool years (ages 0-5), have minimal impairment in sensorimotor areas, and often are not distinguishable from normal children until a later age. By their late teens they can acquire academic skills up to approximately sixth-grade level; during their adult years, they usually achieve social and vocational skills adequate for minimum self-support, but may need guidance and assistance when under unusual social or economic stress. At the present time, virtually all people with Mild Mental Retardation can live successfully in the community, independently or in supervised apartments or group homes (unless there is an associated disorder that makes this impossible).

   b. *Moderate Mental Retardation*

   Moderate Mental Retardation is roughly equivalent to what used to be referred to as the educational category of "trainable." This former term should not be used since it wrongly implies that people with Moderate Mental Retardation cannot benefit from educational programs. This group constitutes 10% of the entire population of people with Mental Retardation.

   Those with this level of Mental Retardation can talk or learn to communicate during the preschool years. They may profit from

27

vocational training and, with moderate supervision, can take care of themselves. They can profit from training in social and occupational skills, but are unlikely to progress beyond the second grade level in academic subjects. They may learn to travel independently in familiar places. During adolescence, their difficulties in recognizing social conventions may interfere with peer relationships. In their adult years, they may be able to contribute to their own support by performing unskilled or semiskilled work under close supervision in sheltered workshops or in the competitive job market. They need supervision and guidance when under stress. They adapt well to life in the community, but usually in supervised group homes.

c. *Severe Mental Retardation*

This group constitutes 3%-4% of people with Mental Retardation. During the pre-school period, they display poor motor development, and they acquire little or no communicative speech. During the school-age period, they may learn to talk, and can be trained in elementary hygiene skills. They profit to only a limited extent from instruction in pre-academic subjects, such as familiarity with the alphabet and simple counting, but can master skills such as learning sight-reading of some "survival" words, such as "men" and "women" and "stop." In their adult years, they may be able to perform simple tasks under close supervision. Most adapt well to life in the community, in group homes or with their families, unless they have an associated handicap that requires specialized nursing or other care.

d. *Profound Mental Retardation*

This group constitutes approximately 1% or 2% of people with Mental Retardation. During the early years, these children display minimal capacity for sensorimotor functioning. A highly structured environment, with constant aid and supervision, and an individualized relationship with a caregiver are required for optimal development. Motor development and self-care and communication skills may improve if appropriate training is provided. Currently, many of these people live in the community, in group homes, intermediate care facilities, or with their families. Most attend day programs, and some can perform simple tasks under close supervision in a sheltered workshop.

C. A Jurisprudence

Two things, first of all, should be observed regarding the classification of the subtypes of mental retardation: that other factors besides IQ are important in determining retardation, and that the IQ itself of a person may differ by as much as twenty points depending on how the person feels when tested. Any rule of thumb in this matter will, therefore, be just that—an approximation.

With that caveat noted, however, it may be said that when a marriage involving a retarded person, even a mildly retarded person, ends in divorce and is presented to a tribunal for adjudication, that marriage may be declared null on the grounds of lack of due discretion.

Indeed, according to a decision coram Rogers of January 31, 1970, not only the retarded person but any person with an IQ below 80 is considered to lack the degree of discretion required for a valid marriage. In that decision, the Rota endorsed the observation of the expert who noted that "an IQ below the 70-80 range is indicative of a pathological condition of mental insufficiency which renders the individual incapable of intending and willing, of administrating one's estate and of conducting business affairs. . . . Substandard intelligence below an IQ of 80 inevitably entails an incapacity to contract marriage." (62, 116-117).

EPILEPSY

A. The Syndrome

1. Definition

   Epilepsy may be defined as a disordered regulation of energy release within the brain entailing the periodic appearance of a recurring pattern of short-lived disturbances of consciousness, typically accompanied by unrestrained motor activity.

   These paroxysmal energy releases or brain storms are called cerebral dysrhythmia and can be measured by an electroencephalogram.

2. Causal and Precipitating Factors

   The dysrhythmia is caused by some brain injury or chemical derangement. It is precipitated by various factors such as alcoholic intake, emotionally charged situations, periods of stress or fatigue, sleep and drowsiness, flickering lights and certain types or tempos of music.

3. Some Specific Epileptic Disorders

   a. The *Grand Mal Seizure* - a major convulsive attack originating in the central integrating system of the higher brain stem. There are four stages in the grand mal seizure:

      1) The Warning Stage - called "auras," involving mood and motor disturbances and visceral sensations and lasting anywhere from a few seconds to a few days.

      2) The Tonic Stage - the period of rigidity lasting less than a minute.

      3) The Clonic Stage - the period of alternating rigidity and relaxation lasting a minute or less.

      4) The Postictal Twilight Stage - the period of automatism lasting anywhere from a few minutes to several days. During this period the subject does not fully regain consciousness, performs automatically and has little or no memory.

   b. *The Ictal Twilight States* - when the brain storms not only originate in the centrencephalic system but also substantially remain there we have an ictal state, sometimes called a psychomotor seizure. Such seizures are of two basic types:

      1) Shorter - lasting for five or ten minutes during which the subject is disoriented and almost totally unaware of his surroundings.

30

2) Longer - lasting several hours or even days during which the subject can mechanically continue previous activities and can appear normal to the casual observer but is, in fact, in a state of automatism or what amounts to a state of unconsciousness.

c. *The Petit Mal Seizure* - a brief attack of impaired consciousness associated with one or more of the following: strong rhythmic blinking of the eyes, nodding of the head, jerking of the arms, sudden loss of posture and staring.

d. *Circumscribed Seizures* - these are motor seizures (eye rolling, masticatory movements, etc.) or sensory seizures (numbness, tingling, buzzing sounds, disagreeable odors, etc.) which do not involve a clouding or loss of consciousness.

e. *Episodic Psychoses* - some epileptics show an extremely variable psychotic symptomatology such as hallucinations, anxiety, ideas of reference, catatonic states, etc. An electroencephalograph, however, can demonstrate that the correct diagnosis is an epileptic episodic psychosis. Furthermore the attacks are generally characterized by some loss of consciousness and by amnesia.

f. *Episodic Psychiatric Changes* - periods of irritableness, depression, mental dullness, lack of initiative, etc. which precede or follow a seizure.

g. *Behavior Disorders* - these are permanent behavioral deviations like emotional rigidity, egoism, hypochrondriasis, verbosity, tendencies to violence, etc. which occur in some epileptics as the result of the same cerebral disorders that cause the convulsions.

B. The Jurisprudence

Besides noting that the typical wedding day (involving fatigue from the preparations, emotional stress of embarking on a new life, extra cocktails, early morning drowsiness, flickering lights and music) is a veritable potpourri of the precipitating factors of epilepsy, few generalizations can be made.

But if we examine the specific epileptic disorders individually, it is clear that some would not be likely to invalidate a marriage while others would.

1. Among the non invalidating types some are too mild, some too severe and some too brief to be sources of nullity.

a. *Too mild* - this would include the warning stage of grand mal seizures, circumscribed seizures, episodic psychiatric changes and most behavior disorders since these latter are normally curable by efficient medication.

b.   *Too severe* - in this category should be listed the tonic and clonic stage of a grand mal which render the person completely unconscious and therefore rule out going through the ceremony.

c.   *Too brief* - the petit mal seizure.

2.   The following three disorders, on the other hand, can easily invalidate a marriage because they rob the subject of the ability even to manifest or express consent since in these states he could not realistically be held accountable for his actions. He is, in short, incapable of placing a human act.

   a.   *Episodic Psychoses*

   These psychoses, even though episodic, may still be considered permanent since the underlying cerebral disorder presumably remains. Even apart from the episodes themselves, therefore, the person is considered psychotic and consequently incapable of marriage.

   b.   *The postictal twilight stage of grand mal*

   This stage, as we have seen, can last for several days. During this time, even though the person may appear calm, he is in fact acting automatically and is not truly in control of, does not truly have dominion over his actions. Any apparent expression of consent would therefore not really express anything deliberate or human.

   c.   *The ictal twilight state*

   This state is, of course, very similar to the postictal stage of the grand mal seizure, particularly in that it is characterized by loss of consciousness and automatism. Furthermore, because this state is not immediately preceded by any seizure that might cause a cancellation of the scheduled marriage and because it can last for several days and also because it can go unnoticed by the casual observer, this ictal state is the epileptic disorder which is most likely to be operative in and indeed invalidating of a marriage.

   In fact, on April 26, 1967, Monsignor Pinna of the Rota gave an affirmative decision in the following case: Julia and George met in school and fell in love. While on an excursion in the Appenine mountains in February of 1948 there was an automobile accident. George was driving and Julia was a passenger along with her brother and two sisters. Julia's head hit the windshield and although her convalescence was brief there were obvious psychic aftereffects. Her personality changed and she began to experience some mind blurring and forgetfulness. In January of 1949, she suffered a blank-spell and in October of 1949, a complete grand mal seizure, followed by several minor disturbances. Despite this, George had relations with her and Julia became pregnant. Then, largely for the sake of the family reputations, they planned to marry in the spring of 1952. According to Julia herself the approaching marriage aggravated her psychic problem, and her memory of the events around the time of the marriage was very hazy. Her mother testified that Julia looked pale while putting on the wedding gown, that she had to lie down for a while and that she looked extremely pale during the ceremony. Other witnesses agreed that she looked foggy and confused.

The marriage proved unhappy. In the spring of 1953 Julia suffered a second grand mal seizure and in November 1954 she fell off a bicycle, apparently during an ictal twilight state.

The couple divorced and George petitioned the Tribunal of Bologna to declare the marriage null. A negative decision was given in the Bologna court and the case eventually went to the Rota.

Several factors are of particular note in this case: that the circumstances preceding and during the wedding tended to trigger or exacerbate Julia's epileptic condition, that Julia underwent a personality change not untypical of the epileptic, that the two grand mal seizures were long before and long after the wedding but that there were apparently rather frequent twilight states in between.

The case was heard "ex automatismo ab epilepsia temporanea" and Pinna concluded that "a sufficient use of reason is removed not only during the ictal stage of a grand mal seizure but in the postictal stage as well and indeed likewise during the ictal twilight state or, as they say, in the state of automatism, because during those periods the mind is beclouded at best and freedom of will reduced practically to zero." (59, 282).

33

ALCOHOLIC INTOXICATION

A. Factors In Intoxication

Basically the degree of intoxication depends on the percentage of alcohol in the bloodstream which, in turn, depends on several factors. Among these factors are:

1. *Intake Duration*

   Some alcohol is eliminated in the urine and by perspiration but most of it, about 90% of it, must be oxidized or burned off in the liver. The liver, however, can only burn alcohol at a fixed rate of something less than one ounce per hour of 100 proof liquor so if a person consumes a great deal of alcohol in a short period of time the alcohol accumulates in the blood.

2. *Absorption*

   The bloodstream absorbs from the intestines more quickly than it does from the stomach so that if the stomach is filled with food the absorption of alcohol is delayed. Furthermore, wine and beer contain food elements within themselves and are therefore more slowly absorbed than other alcoholic beverages.

3. *Tolerance*

   Exhaustion, emotional stress and other factors can lower one's tolerance to alcohol and besides, some people seem to have a kind of psychological tolerance to alcohol which permits them to ingest fairly large amounts of alcohol without becoming intoxicated.

4. *Weight*

   The size and weight of a person is a considerable factor in intoxication. Generally speaking, a 200 pound person can drink twice as much as a 100 pound person before reaching the same blood alcohol level.

5. *Amount of Alcohol*

   This obviously is the principal factor in intoxication. Recognizing that the factors mentioned above can modify the results, the following table, based on a 160 pound person drinking 90 proof whiskey, is, nevertheless, generally reliable.

   a. Two ounces dulls the top layers of the brain, causes some diminution in inhibition and in recognizing conventional courtesy and results in a blood alcohol level (bal) of .05%.

b. Four ounces affects the moral and physical control centers, often motivates the person to take certain liberties and results in a bal of .10%, recognized by many states in the U.S. as constituting legal drunkenness.

c. Six ounces causes blurred speech and unsteady gait, slows reflexes, causes carelessness, over confidence and impulsive behavior and results in a bal of .15%, recognized by all states as constituting legal drunkenness.

d. Eight ounces affects the lower motor and sensory areas of the brain, causes double vision and drowsiness and results in a bal of .20%.

e. Ten ounces causes increasingly slower reflexes, poorer judgment and results in a bal of .25%.

f. Twelve ounces results in lurching unsteadiness during which the person needs help to walk or undress and tends to fall asleep. Results in a bal of .30%.

g. Fourteen ounces affects the more primitive areas of the brain, causes the person to lose practically all consciousness and fall into a stupor. Bal - .35% or more.

B. A Jurisprudence

1. In general, where the person both consents to marry and also actually goes through the marriage ceremony during the period of intoxication, then *imperfect* drunkeness suffices to invalidate the marriage. But *perfect* drunkenesss is required to invalidate the marriage when the person has already consented and agreed to marry but gets drunk on the day of the wedding in order to get through the ceremony itself (47, 383).

2. More specifically, the standard commentators on moral theology customarily defined the signs of *perfect* drunkenness as an inability to distinguish right from wrong, an inability to remember the major events of the preceding day and an entirely unaccustomed mode of behavior; whereas the signs of *imperfect* drunkenness were such things as double vision, unsteady gait, dizziness and vomiting (Noldin-Schmidt, 1, 339).

3. In terms of percentage of alcohol in the blood stream, this means that a blood alcohol level of from .15% to .20% would constitute *imperfect* drunkenness and would incapacitate a person for *giving* consent. And a blood alcohol level of .25% to .30% would constitute *perfect* drunkenness and incapacitate the person for *expressing* consent.

4. The court should, moreover, be alert to the possibility, where a person was heavily intoxicated at the time of the ceremony, of other sources of nullity. The person, for example, might have become intoxicated in order to get through a ceremony which he or she was thoroughly unwilling to enter anyway and which might have involved force or simulation.

35

IDENTITY DISORDER

A. The Syndrome

DSM III R describes the Identity Disorder as follows:

1. *Essential Feature*

    The essential feature of this disorder is severe subjective distress regarding inability to integrate aspects of the self into a relatively coherent and acceptable sense of self. There is uncertainty about a variety of issues relating to identity, including long-term goals, career choice, friendship patterns, sexual orientation and behavior, religious identification, moral value systems, and group loyalties. These symptoms last at least three months and result in impairment in social or occupational (including academic) functioning. The disturbance does not occur exclusively during the course of another mental disorder, such as a Mood Disorder, Schizophrenia, or Schizophreniform Disorder; the disturbance is not sufficiently pervasive and persistent to warrant the diagnosis of Borderline Personality Disorder.

    The uncertainty regarding long-term goals may be expressed as inability to choose or adopt a life pattern, for example, one dedicated to material success, or service to the community, or even some combination of the two. Conflict regarding career choice may be expressed as inability to decide on a career or as inability to pursue an apparently chosen occupation. Conflict regarding friendship patterns may be expressed in an inability to decide the kinds of people with whom to be friendly and the degree of intimacy to permit. Conflict regarding values and loyalties may include concerns about religious identification, patterns of sexual behavior, and oral issues. The person experiences these conflicts as irreconcilable aspects of his or her personality and, as a result, fails to perceive himself or herself as having a coherent identity. Frequently the disturbance is epitomized by the person's asking, "Who am I?"

2. *Associated Features*

    Mild anxiety and depression are common and are usually related to inner preoccupations rather than external events. Self-doubt and doubt about the future are usually present, and take the form of either difficulty in making choices or impulsive experimentation. Negative or oppositional patterns are often chosen in an attempt to establish an independent identity distinct from family or other close people. Such attempts may include transient experimental phases of widely divergent bahavior as the person "tries on" various roles.

3. *Age At Onset*

    The most common age at onset is late adolescence, when people generally become detached from their family value systems and attempt to establish independent identities. As value systems change, this disorder may also appear in young adulthood,or even in middle age, if a person begins to question earlier life decisions.

4. *Course*

Frequently there is a phase with acute onset, which either resolves over a period of time or becomes chronic. In other instances the onset is more gradual. If the disorder begins in adolescence, it is usually resolved by the mid-20s. If it becomes chronic, however, the person may be unable to make a career commitment, or may fail to form lasting emotional attachments, with resulting frequent shifts in jobs, relationships, and career directions.

B. A Jurisprudence

Everyone agrees that fourteen and fifteen year old children in our culture lack the due discretion for marriage. They perhaps enjoy sufficient *knowledge* to enter marriage, that is, they are not ignorant that marriage is a permanent partnership between man and woman, ordered to the procreation of children through some sexual cooperation. But they do not enjoy sufficient *maturity* or discretion to be able to evaluate those notions as they might apply, in practice, to themselves.

Given the proper circumstances, these young people should, over the next several years, develop sufficient discretion to be able to enter marriage validly. Gradually they should come to know themselves and be able to judge other people, so that eventually they reach the point where they are able to make a reasonably sound, prudent judgment about sharing their life with another specific human being in a partnership of life that involves self revelation, understanding and loving and which includes the procreation and education of children.

Oftentimes, however, normal development is arrested by the disorder here described, with the result that some young people who are biologically nineteen or twenty are psychologically only fourteen or fifteen, and therefore lack the due discretion for marriage.

When a Court is asked to investigate the validity of a marriage which was entered by a young person and later failed, attention should be paid to the possibility that the marriage was null because of lack of due discretion.

The Court should attempt to assess whether the decision to marry was at least minimally prudential, whether the critical faculty was truly at work, whether due discretion was present. A profile of the person's general behavior pattern should be obtained; was there excessive reliance on parents? was the party capable generally of making independent decisions? were values adopted simply because parents or parental figures opposed them? were peer relationships markedly dependent? was the person seeing himself as one fairly consistent person? was he plagued with doubts about himself and about the future? was there impulsive behavior? experimentation? etc.?

If it is clear to the Court that psychologically, the person was, in effect, stalled in early adolescence, still struggling with the conflicts of that period, and therefore not yet come up to an acceptable level of maturity necessary to enter the demanding, lifelong covenant of marriage, it may be concluded that the marriage was null because of lack of due discretion.

PRESSURED CONSENT

The law on force and fear is well known. In order to be invalidating it must be grave, extrinsic, and causative.

Over the years some authors have suggested that the requirement of extrinsicality is excessive, and that fear should be regarded as invalidating even when there is no extrinsic force. Given the human condition, they say, the source of the fear, i.e. whether it be extrinsic or intrinsic, is not all that important. Intrinsic fear can be just as severe and just as paralyzing as extrinsic fear.

Generally, however, jurists have seen wisdom in the traditional approach. The ground of "vis et metus" is designed for application to a specific situation, namely one where there is not only "metus" but also "vis," that is to say, some extrinsic force. Where such a situation is not verified, one should look to another ground.

This seems fair enough. Particularly considering the fact that the adjacent ground of lack of due discretion picks up exactly where force and fear leaves off. Where, in other words, the fear is present to such a degree that it disturbs the subject's faculties and disables him from making a sound judgment and a free choice, then, even though the fear is intrinsic, the marriage is nevertheless invalid, not on the grounds of force and fear but on the grounds of lack of due discretion.

Given sufficient pressures, even mature, experienced people can make stupid, disastrous mistakes. The ship's captain, for example, when suddenly faced with another ship bearing down on him from out of the fog, and with only a split second to make a decision, turns port instead of starboard. The ships collide and lives are lost. He might spend the rest of his life wondering why he failed to make the obvious and traditional turn to starboard, but the fact is that the pressure was so great that it robbed him of his wits.

Lesser pressure has the same effect on lesser people. Immature, inexperienced people can be robbed of their wits by a circumstance that would be quite manageable for the average person.

When all of this is applied to marriage, it can be said that, given sufficient pressure on a sufficiently immature person, the faculties of intellect and will can be so diminished as to render marital consent defective and the marriage null. To be more specific, it is entirely conceivable, and surely recognised by the principles of our jurisprudence, that when a young, immature girl discovers that she is pregnant, given certain attitudes on her part, and a certain attachment to her family, and given a certain amount of pressure, which may fall short of the "vis" required in a force and fear case, and given, on the one hand, a certain time limit within which to make a decision, and, on the other hand, a protraction of the pressure, it is, I repeat, entirely conceivable that such a girl could, so to speak, turn port into marriage rather than starboard away from it. She could, in other words, be robbed of her wits, temporarily deprived of due discretion and thus enter marriage irresponsibly and invalidly.

LACK OF DUE COMPETENCE

GENERAL REMARKS

A. The Pertinent Canon

C. 1095   - They are incapable of contracting marriage
   3° - who are not strong enough to assume the essential obligations of matrimony due to causes of a psychic nature.

B. The Context Of The Canon

This 3° of C. 1095 (on lack of due *competence*) is perhaps best understood in conjunction with 1° (on lack of due *reason*) and 2° (on lack of due *discretion*). These read as follows:

C. 1095   - They are incapable of contracting marriage
   1° - who lack the sufficient use of reason
   2° - who suffer from grave lack of discretion of judgment concerning essential matrimonial rights and duties which are to be mutually given and accepted.

C. The Meaning Of Incompetence

1. Lack of due competence (sometimes referred to as "marital incompetence" or simply "incompetence") is the disability for assuming the essential obligations of marriage.

2. It is, first of all, a disability. The canon notes that some psychological reason brings it about that the person is not strong enough, i.e. the psychological reason deprives him of the necessary psychic resources, i.e. it disables him. He is unable because he has been weakened; his strength has been impaired.

3. The canon further notes that the impairment involves an inability to *assume* the essential obligations of marriage. The question arises, however: how does one decide whether a person is unable to *assume* obligations? In practice, a judge usually investigates the matter indirectly. The direct, immediate object of the judge's investigation is the ability or inability of the party to *fulfill* the obligations of marriage. The judge looks to the behavior, the performance of the person before and after marriage. If the conclusion is reached that the person *did not fulfill* essential responsibilities and indeed *could not,* the judge then goes on to conclude that the person was unable to *assume* those obligations, since it is axiomatic that one cannot *assume* what one cannot *fulfill.*

4. Why, then, does the Code speak about the indirect question (the inability to *assume*) rather than the direct question (the inability to *fulfill*)? It does so,

partly at least, because it wishes to emphasize that the fundamental defect, even in a lack of due competence case, is a consensual one. This too is why C. 1095 is positioned where it is, in Chapter IV - On Matrimonial Consent.

5. In practice, therefore, a judge concentrates his investigation on the *matrimonium in facto esse* (the relationship) but, in theory, the invalidating factor devolves to the *matrimonium in fieri* (the covenanting). See 68, 387 and D2, p. 64.

6. Along these same lines, Navarrete (in *Periodica,* 1972, p. 53) made a useful distinction in pointing out that, unlike the lack of due reason and discretion case, which involves a true incapacity for placing consent (*incapacitas praestandi consensum*), the lack of due competence case is more a matter of an incapacity for placing the object of consent (*incapacitas praestandi objectum consensus*).

D. The Object Of Incompetence

1. The object of incompetence is the essential obligations of marriage. It is when a person is disabled from assuming these obligations that he or she is incapable of contracting marriage.

2. These obligations stem, of course, from the nature of marriage as a "covenant by which a man and a woman establish between them a partnership of their entire lives, a partnership which is, by its very nature, ordered to the good of the spouses and to the procreation and education of children" (C. 1055 §1).

3. These essential obligations of marriage are basically twofold: procreational and personalist.

    When a person is incapable of assuming the *procreational* obligations of marriage he or she is said to be impotent, as regulated by C. 1084.

    As regards the *personalist* obligations, these are those actions which are required in order to sustain the marital partnership "which is, by its very nature, ordered to the good of the spouses." As C. 1135 says, "Each of the spouses has equal obligations and rights to those things which pertain to the partnership of conjugal life." More specifically, these "essential obligations" of marriage consist in:

    a. *Self Revelation* - a person must first of all enjoy a basic ego identity, i.e. he must see himself as one fairly consistent person, have a reasonable degree of respect for that person, and convey a knowledge of himself to his spouse.

    b. *Understanding* - a person must see his spouse as a separate person, and appreciate her way of feeling and thinking, without distorting it excessively by his own attitudes, needs or insecurities.

41

c. *Loving* - a person must be capable of being a loving person to his spouse, i.e. he must be able to give to his spouse and to receive from her an affection that bonds them as a couple.

Both spouses, furthermore, must have the ability to perform these same three acts towards any children that might be born of the marriage, since marriage "by its very nature, is ordered to the procreation and education of children."

When a person lacks the ability to perform those acts, and therefore lacks the ability to assume those obligations, he or she is said to lack the due competence for marriage, as marriage is understood in the Catholic community.

For a valid marriage, it is not necessary that a person actually perform those acts, but it is necessary that he have the capacity to perform those acts and that he exchange the perpetual right to them.

E. The Term Incompetence

If one sees impotence as an incapacity, then incapacity for assuming the essential obligations of marriage is a genus of which there are two species: 1) *impotence,* the incapacity for the procreational obligations of marriage (regarded as an impediment) and 2) *incompetence,* the incapacity for the personalist obligations of marriage (regarded as a defect of consent).

The Rota and many other courts refer to the ground of nullity described in C. 1095, 3° as "incapacity for assuming the essential obligations of marriage." To this author, however, it seems more precise to use the specific rather than the generic term, that is, to call this ground incompetence (or lack of due competence) rather than incapacity.

F. The Causes Of Incompetence

1. C. 1095, unlike earlier drafts of the canon, does not concern itself with specific causes of the various defects. It says nothing at all about the causes behind lack of due reason and lack of due discretion, and regarding lack of due competence, it merely notes that some psychological reasons (causae naturae psychicae) would bring it about.

2. The phrase "psychological reasons" is, obviously, extremely broad and would include psychoses, neuroses, personality disorders and even homosexuality, which the American Psychiatric Association does not regard as a disorder unless it happens to be ego-dystonic, i.e. unless the person is consistently concerned about changing his or her sexual orientation. The phrase could also include the situation where neither party to the marriage suffers from a true disorder but they still remain truly incapable of establishing a marital relationship with each other. See the decision of April 5, 1973 coram Serrano, paragraph 7 in D1, p. 12.

3. For further specifics regarding the causes of incompetence, see Section H on the areas of investigation.

G. The Result Of Incompetence

As noted in Section C, 4, 5 and 6, lack of due competence is *au fond,* a defect of consent. Unlike impotence, therefore, incompetence is regarded in law not as an impediment but rather as an inability to elicit consent. See Section B in the chapters on Impotence.

H. Areas Of Investigation

When investigating lack of due competence, four areas deserve particular attention: severity, antecedence, perpetuity and relativity.

1. *Severity.* The "psychological reasons" of which the canon speaks must be, to some extent, disabling. They must, in other words, bring it about that the party or parties were not strong enough (non valent - for a somewhat similar use of the term see C. 689 §3) to assume the essential obligations of marriage. This implies some degree of severity. Generally speaking, there-fore, "mild characterological disturbances," as DiFelice noted (D2, p. 65) would not be regarded as disabling. Some rotal auditors, as a matter of fact, consider it a rule of thumb that only an incurable disorder can be considered serious enough to be invalidating. See McGrath, Aidan "On the Gravity of Causes of a Psychological Nature in the Proof of Inability to Assume the Essential Obligations of Marriage," *Studia Canonica* 22/1, 1988, pp. 71-72.

2. *Antecedence.* The disability in question is that of *assuming* the obligations of marriage. One, of course, assumes these obligations at the moment of marriage. To be invalidating, in other words, the disability must exist at the moment of marriage, that is to say , it must be antecedent to (or at least concomitant with) the consent to marry.

   This is not to say, however, that the incompetence should have manifested itself beforehand. It is not required that the incompetence be actual or dynamic at the time of marriage, but only that it be virtual or causal. It is necessary and it suffices that the proximate disposition to incompetence and the proximate causes of its onset be present at the time of marriage.

   For example, a woman with a severe Personality Disorder enters marriage. For a time she functions adequately in marriage but after six months or a year the disorder surfaces, severely impairs her ability to meet her obligations, and destroys the marriage. Such a woman would be regarded as virtually or causally incompetent because a Personality Disorder, by its nature as a pervasive personality pattern, is *present* from childhood or at least adolescence, even though it might not be *apparent* at the time of marriage.

3. *Perpetuity.* Since perpetuity is one of the essential properties of marriage (CC. 1056 and 1134), it follows that the essential obligations of marriage are

lifelong obligations. In order to enter a valid marriage, therefore, it is not enough that a person has the capacity to assume the obligations for a month or a year or a decade; it is, rather, required that one have the capacity, at the time of marriage, to assume the perpetual obligations involved in marriage.

Clearly this is quite different from the perpetuity that must be proved in an impotence case.

In a case of impotence it is the incapacity which must be perpetual. In order to be invalidating, in other words, the impotence must exist throughout the entire marriage, from beginning to end and even beyond. If, therefore, a man lived in a marriage for five years and was capable of intercourse only for the first year, say, or only for the last, that marriage could not be proved null on the grounds of impotence because the impotence was not perpetual. Temporary impotence is not invalidating. In the case of impotence, therefore, the requirement of perpetuity makes it harder to prove invalidity. The requirement of perpetuity favors validity.

In the case of incompetence, however, it is quite different. Here it is not the incapacity but the obligations that are perpetual. Unlike impotence, incompetence can invalidate even though it is not perpetual. Consider again the woman who enters marriage with a severe Personality Disorder. She functions reasonably well for, say, a year but then the Disorder surfaces and destroys the marriage over the next three or four years. Or perhaps the Disorder causes destructive behavior right from the beginning and the husband finds it intolerable after a year and leaves; had he stayed for three or four years it is possible that the woman could have entered therapy and modified her behavior but in fact the Disorder destroyed the marriage before the Disorder could be controlled. In both cases the marriage can be declared null because in both cases the woman was incapable of assuming the perpetual obligations of marriage. In the case of incompetence, therefore, the requirement of perpetuity (that is, the fact that the obligations undertaken are perpetual) makes it easier to prove invalidity. The requirement of perpetuity favors nullity (in the sense that perpetual obligations are more demanding than temporary obligations).

The position taken by the author on this point (namely that perpetuity refers not to the incapacity but to the obligations) is but one of several positions taken by jurists over the last several years. For a brief discussion of these positions see Fellhauer, David *The New Code of Canon Law, Proceedings of the 5th International Congress,* II, pp. 1036-37 and *CLSA Proceedings, 1986,* pp. 111-112.

It should be noted however, that for a marriage to be considered invalid, the spouse in question must truly be incompetent at the time of marriage and not just become so later on. It might happen, for example, that at the time of marriage, a man suffers from a mild or moderate Personality Disorder. At the time he is aware of the value and need of therapy but neglects to avail himself of it. Unattended, the disorder is exacerbated by the stresses of marriage and becomes severe and destructive. Since it was curable, that is to say, controllable at the time of marriage, the man would not be regarded as incompetent.

4. *Relativity.* Sometimes incompetence is *absolute* (where the person would be incapable of marrying anyone), but sometimes it is *relative* (where the person is judged incapable of entering a relationship with the particular partner he in fact chose as his spouse). It is important, therefore, that a person's competence always be judged relative to the marriage in question and not just in general. It may even happen in a given instance that the only identifiable, diagnosable disorder present consists in the inability of the person to engage in the marital relationship in question. But since every marriage is essentially a relationship, where there is no capacity for the relationship there is no marriage. See the Serrano decision of 4/5/73 as found in D1, p. 8.

This position, it should be noted, is not endorsed by all jurists. Pompedda, for example, denies that there is any genuine foundation in jurisprudence for the notion of relative incapacity. See Pompedda, Mario, "Incapacity to Assume the Essential Obligations of Marriage" in *Incapacity For Marriage,* Third Gregorian Colloquium, Robert Sable, coodinator and editor, Rome, 1987, pp. 205-206.

I. Proof Of Lack Of Due Competence

1. *Parties, Affiants and Witnesses*

   In cases involving an alleged lack of due competence every effort should be made to obtain testimony from the respondent (usually the party whose incompetence is alleged). Sometimes the petitioner has lost touch with the respondent, and cannot provide an address, but usually, with a little effort, the respondent can be located.

   The declarations of the parties and the affidavits and testimony of others are extremely important in these cases since they provide the data on which a judgment can be made. For the canons pertaining to the evaluation of this evidence, see one of the four chapters on simulation (total simulation, intentions against children, fidelity and perpetuity) in the section on proof.

2. *Experts*

   a. *The Law*

      C. 1680 reads as follows: In cases of impotence or defect of consent due to mental illness, the judge is to use the services of one or more experts unless it is obvious from the circumstances that this would be useless; in other cases the prescription of C. 1574 is to be observed.

C. 1574 says: The services of experts must be used whenever their examination and opinion, based on the laws of art or science, are required in order to establish some fact or to clarify the true nature of some thing by reason of a prescription of the law or a judge.

b.   *An Observation*

C. 1680 notes that an expert is called when 1) there is a defect of consent and 2) there is a mentis morbus.

Lack of due competence, as noted under G, does involve a defect of consent. The term "mentis morbus" is here translated "mental illness" or "mental disorder" because, since the first edition of the *Diagnostic and Statistical Manual* in 1952, the American Psychiatric Association has referred to all psychopathology as Mental Disorders. For practical purposes here in America, therefore, the term may be regarded as coextensive with the disorders listed in DSM III R.

A lack of due competence case, as noted in F, does not always involve a mental disorder. Sometimes, for example, the incompetence is caused by homosexuality (which is not, per se, a disorder) or by a non-pathological incapacity for the particular relationship in question. In such cases the services of an expert would be at the discretion of the judge. It is only when a true disorder is present that a perital report is required.

c.   *The Probative Force*

C. 1579 §1 says that the judge is to weigh attentively not only the conclusions of the experts but also the other circumstances of the case. This is a reminder that the judge is the *peritus peritorum* and that, besides the report of the expert, the judge must also be concerned with such questions as whether the data on which the conclusions of the expert are based are truly proved by the evidence. It is in this sense that the *dicta peritorum cribranda sunt,* i.e., that the report of the expert should be "sifted." At the same time, however, *peritis in arte credendum est* and, as Parisella noted, "When it comes to evaluating the weight and importance of the expert's report, the Rota has many times (see the decisions of 10/21/59 coram Lamas, of 8/5/54 coram Pinna, of 11/6/56 coram Mattioli, of 2/26/52 and 4/6/54 coram Felici) taught that it is wrong for the judge to depart from the conclusions of the experts except for very weighty contrary arguments." (60, 564-565).

J.   Use Of The Ground

It often happens that a person lacks both due competence and due discretion. In such a case a tribunal is free to select the ground on the basis of the particular circumstances. It may happen, for example, that the woman in a case is diagnosed by the expert as suffering from a Narcissistic Personality Disorder. If the woman was twenty-five years old at the time of the marriage and was married after a two year courtship, the court would be inclined to judge the case on the grounds of lack of due *competence*. If, however, the woman was sixteen and pregnant and married after a five month courtship, the court would be inclined to judge the case on the ground of lack of due *discretion*. The same is true of other disorders. Anxiety Disorders, Mood Disorders and Schizophrenia, for example, are often heard as Lack of Due Discretion rather than Lack of Due Competence cases, depending on the circumstances as well as on the jurisprudential convictions of the judge. See also D2, p. 65.

PERSONALITY DISORDERS

A. Description

DSM III R describes Personality Disorders as follows:

1. *General Remarks*

   Personality *traits* are enduring patterns of perceiving, relating to, and thinking about the environment and oneself, and are exhibited in a wide range of important social and personal contexts. It is only when *personality traits* are inflexible and maladaptive and cause either significant functional impairment or subjective distress that they constitute *Personality Disorders.* The manifestations of Personality Disorders are often recognizable by adolescence or earlier and continue throughout most of adult life, though they often become less obvious in middle or old age.

2. *Associated Features*

   Frequently the person with a Personality Disorder is dissatisfied with the impact his or her behavior is having on others or with his or her inability to function effectively. This may be the case even when the traits that lead to these difficulties are ego-syntonic, that is, are not regarded by the person as undesirable. In other cases, the traits may be ego-dystonic, but the person may be unable to modify them despite great effort.

   Disturbances of mood, frequently involving depression or anxiety, are common, and may even be the person's chief complaint.

3. *Age at Onset and Course*

   As noted above, Personality Disorders by definition generally are recognizable by adolescence or early adult life and are characteristic of most of adult life.

4. *Impairment*

   There may be marked impairment in social and occupational functioning. When occupational functioning is impaired, the impairment is usually sustained, but may be episodic and take the form of recurrent periods of work inhibition (e.g., "writer's block"). With the exception of Antisocial, Schizotypal, and Borderline Personality Disorders, people with Personality Disorders rarely require hospitalization unless there is a superimposed disorder, such as a Psychoactive Substance Use Disorder or Major Depression.

B. Subtypes

DSM III R has grouped Personality Disorders into three clusters. The first cluster,

48

referred to as cluster A, includes Paranoid, Schizoid, and Schizotypal Personality Disorders. People with these disorders often appear odd or eccentric. Cluster B includes Antisocial, Borderline, Histrionic, and Narcissistic Personality Disorders. People with these disorders often appear dramatic, emotional, or erratic. Cluster C includes Avoidant, Dependent, Obsessive Compulsive, and Passive Aggressive Personality Disorders. People with these disorders often appear anxious or fearful. Finally, there is a residual category, Personality Disorder Not Otherwise Specified, that can be used for other Specific Personality Disorders or for mixed conditions that do not qualify as any of the specific Personality Disorders described in this manual.

1.   Cluster A (Odd or Eccentric)

   a.   Paranoid

      1)   *Essential Feature*

         The essential feature of this disorder is a pervasive and unwarranted tendency, beginning by early adulthood and present in a variety of contexts, to interpret the actions of people as deliberately demeaning or threatening.

         Almost invariably there is a general expectation of being exploited or harmed by others in some way. Frequently a person with this disorder will question, without justification, the loyalty or trustworthiness of friends or associates. Often the person is pathologically jealous, questioning without justification the fidelity of his or her spouse or sexual partner.

         Confronted with a new situation, the person may read hidden demeaning or threatening meanings into benign remarks or events, e.g., suspect that a bank has deliberately made a mistake in his account. Often these people are easily slighted and quick to react with anger or counterattack; they may bear grudges for a long time, and never forgive slights, insults, or injuries. They are reluctant to confide in others because of a fear that the information will be used against them. People with this disorder are typically hypervigilant and take precautions against any perceived threat. They tend to avoid blame even when it is warranted. They are often viewed by others as guarded, secretive, devious, and scheming.

         When people with this disorder find themselves in a new situation, they intensely and narrowly search for confirmation of their expectations, with no appreciation of the total context. Their final conclusion is usually precisely what they expected in the first place. Often, they have transient ideas of reference, e.g., that others are taking special notice of them, or saying vulgar things about them.

People with this disorder are usually argumentative and exaggerate difficulties, "making mountains out of molehills." They often find it difficult to relax, usually appear tense, and have a tendency to counterattack when they perceive any threat. Though they are critical of others, and often litigious, they have great difficulty accepting criticism themselves.

The affectivity of these people is often restricted, and they may appear "cold" to others. They have no true sense of humor and are usually serious. They may pride themselves on always being objective, rational, and unemotional. They usually lack passive, soft, sentimental, and tender feelings.

Occasionally, others see people with this disorder as keen observers who are energetic, ambitious, and capable; but more often they are viewed as hostile, stubborn, and defensive. They tend to be rigid and unwilling to compromise, and may generate uneasiness and fear in others. They often have an inordinate fear of losing their independence or the power to shape events according to their own wishes.

These people usually avoid intimacy except with those in whom they have absolute trust. They display an excessive need to be self-sufficient, to the point of egocentricity and exaggerated self-importance. They avoid participation in group activities unless they are in a dominant position.

People with Paranoid Personality Disorder are often interested in mechanical devices, electronics, and automation. They are generally uninterested in art or aesthetics. They are keenly aware of power and rank and of who is superior or inferior, and are often envious and jealous of those in positions of power. They disdain people they see as weak, soft, sickly, or defective.

During periods of extreme stress, people with this disorder may experience transient psychotic symptoms, but they are usually of insufficient duration to warrant an additional diagnosis.

b. Schizoid

1) *Essential Feature*

The essential feature of this disorder is a pervasive pattern of indifference to social relationships and a restricted range of emotional experience and expression, beginning by early adulthood and present in a variety of contexts.

People with this disorder neither desire nor enjoy close relationships, including being part of a family. They prefer to be "loners," and have no close friends or confidants (or only one) other than first-degree relatives. They almost always choose solitary activities and indicate little if any desire to have sexual experiences with another person. Such people are indifferent to the praise and criticism of others. They claim that they rarely experience strong emotions such as anger and joy, and in fact display a constricted affect. They appear cold and aloof.

2) *Associated Features*

People with this disorder are often unable to express aggressiveness or hostility. They may seem vague about their goals, indecisive in their actions, self-absorbed, and absentminded. Because of a lack of social skills or desire for sexual experiences, males with this disorder are usually incapable of dating and rarely marry. Females may passively accept courtship and marry.

c. Schizotypal

1) *Essential Feature*

The essential feature of this disorder is a pervasive pattern of peculiarities of ideation, appearance, and behavior and deficits in interpersonal relatedness, beginning by early adulthood and present in a variety of contexts, that are not severe enough to meet the criteria for Schizophrenia.

The disturbance in the content of thought may include paranoid ideation, suspiciousness, ideas of reference, odd beliefs, and magical thinking that is inconsistent with subcultural norms and influences the person's behavior. Examples include superstitiousness, belief in clairvoyance, telepathy, or "sixth sense," or beliefs that "others can feel my feelings" (when it is not part of a cultural belief system). In children and adolescents, these thoughts may include bizarre fantasies or preoccupations. Unusual perceptual experiences may include illusions and sensing the presence of a force or person not actually present (e.g., "I felt an evil presence in the room"). Often speech shows marked peculiarities, but never to the point of loosening of associations or incoherence. Speech may be impoverished, digressive, vague, or inappropriately abstract. Concepts may be expressed unclearly or oddly, or words may be used in an unusual way. People with this disorder often appear odd and eccentric in behavior and appearance. For example, they are often unkempt, display unusual mannerisms, and talk to themselves.

Interpersonal relatedness is invariably impaired in these people. They display inappropriate or constricted affect, appearing silly and aloof and rarely reciprocating gestures or facial expressions, such as smiling or nodding. They have no close friends or confidants (or only one) other than first-degree relatives, and are extremely anxious in social situations involving unfamiliar people.

2) *Associated Features*

Varying mixtures of anxiety, depression, and other dysphoric moods are common. Features of Borderline Personality Disorder are often present, and in some cases both diagnoses may be warranted. During periods of extreme stress, people with this disorder may experience transient psychotic symptoms, but they are usually insufficient in duration to warrant an additional diagnosis. Because of peculiarities in thinking, people with Schizo-typal Personality Disorder are prone to eccentric convictions.

2. Cluster B (Dramatic, Emotional or Erratic)

   a. Antisocial

   1) *Essential Feature*

   The essential feature of this disorder is a pattern of irresponsible and antisocial behavior beginning in childhood or early adoles-cence and continuing into adulthood. For this diagnosis to be given, the person must be at least 18 years of age and have a history of Conduct Disorder before the age of 15.

   Lying, stealing, truancy, vandalism, initiating fights, running away from home, and physical cruelty are typical childhood signs. In adulthood the antisocial pattern continues, and may include failure to honor financial obligations, to function as a responsible parent or to plan ahead, and an inability to sustain consistent work behavior. These people fail to conform to social norms and repeatedly perform antisocial acts that are grounds for arrest, such as destroying property, harassing others, stealing, and having an illegal occupation.

   People with Antisocial Personality Disorder tend to be irritable and aggressive and to get repeatedly into physical fights and assaults, including spouse- or child-beating. Reckless behavior without regard to personal safety is common, as indicated by frequently driving while intoxicated or getting speeding tickets. Typically, these people are promiscuous (defined as never having sustained a monogamous relationship for more than a year). Finally, they generally have no remorse about the effects of their behavior on others; they may even feel justified in having hurt or mistreated others. After age 30, the more flagrantly antisocial behavior may diminish, particularly sexual promiscuity, fighting, and criminality.

2) *Associated Features*

In early adolescence these people characteristically use tobacco, alcohol, and other drugs and engage in voluntary sexual intercourse unusually early for their peer group. Psychoactive Substance Use Disorders are commonly associated diagnoses. Less commonly, Somatization Disorder may be present.

Despite the stereotype of a normal mental status in this disorder, frequently there are signs of personal distress, including complaints of tension, inability to tolerate boredom, depression, and the conviction (often correct) that others are hostile toward them. The interpersonal difficulties and dysphoria tend to persist into late adult life even when the more flagrant antisocial behavior has diminished. Almost invariably there is a markedly impaired capacity to sustain lasting, close, warm, and responsible relationships with family, friends, or sexual partners.

b.   Borderline

1) *Essential Feature*

The essential feature of this disorder is a pervasive pattern of instability of self-image, interpersonal relationships, and mood, beginning by early adulthood and present in a variety of contexts.

A marked and persistent identity disturbance is almost invariably present. This is often pervasive, and is manifested by uncertainty about several life issues, such as self-image, sexual orientation, long-term goals or career choice, types of friends or lovers to have, or which values to adopt. The person often experiences this instability of self-image as chronic feelings of emptiness or boredom.

Interpersonal relationships are usually unstable and intense, and may be characterized by alternation of the extremes of over-idealization and devaluation. These people have difficulty tolerating being alone, and will make frantic efforts to avoid real or imagined abandonment.

Affective instability is common. This may be evidenced by marked mood shifts from baseline mood to depression, irritability, or anxiety, usually lasting a few hours or, only rarely, more than a few days. In addition, these people often have inappropriately intense anger or lack of control of their anger, with frequent displays of temper or recurrent physical fights. They tend to be impulsive, particularly in activities that are potentially self-damaging, such as shopping sprees, psychoactive substance abuse, reckless driving, casual sex, shoplifting, and binge eating.

Recurrent suicidal threats, gestures, or behavior and other self-mutilating behavior (e.g., wrist-scratching) are common in the more severe forms of the disorder. This behavior may serve to manipulate others, may be a result of intense anger, or may counteract feelings of "numbness" and depersonalization that arise during periods of extreme stress.

Some conceptualize this disorder as a level of personality organization rather than as a specific Personality Disorder.

2) *Associated Features*

Frequently this disorder is accompanied by many features of other Personality Disorders, such as Schizotypal, Histrionic, Narcissistic, and Antisocial Personality Disorders. In many cases more than one diagnosis is warranted. Quite often social contrariness and a generally pessimistic outlook are observed. Alternation between dependency and self-assertion is common. During periods of extreme stress, transient psychotic symptoms may occur, but they are generally of insufficient severity or duration to warrant an additional diagnosis.

c. Histrionic

1) *Essential Feature*

The essential feature of this disorder is a pervasive pattern of excessive emotionality and attention-seeking, beginning by early adulthood and present in a variety of contexts. In other classifications this category is termed Hysterical Personality.

People with this disorder constantly seek or demand reassurance, approval, or praise from others and are uncomfortable in situations in which they are not the center of attention. They characteristically display rapidly shifting and shallow expression of emotions. Their behavior is overly reactive and intensely expressed; minor stimuli give rise to emotional excitability. Emotions are often expressed with inappropriate exaggeration, for example, the person may appear much more sad, angry, or delighted than would seem to be warranted. People with this disorder tend to be very self-centered, with little or no tolerance for the frustration of delayed gratification. Their actions are directed to obtaining immediate satisfaction.

These people are typically attractive and seductive, often to the point of looking flamboyant and acting inappropriately. They are typically overly concerned with physical attractiveness. In addition, their style of speech tends to be expressionistic and lacking in detail. For example, a person may describe his vacation as "Just fantastic!" without being able to be more specific.

2) *Associated Features*

People with this disorder are lively and dramatic and are always drawing attention to themselves. They are prone to exaggeration in their interpersonal relations and often act out a role such as that of "victim" or "princess" without being aware of it. They crave novelty, stimulation, and excitement and quickly become bored with normal routine. Others frequently perceive them as superficially charming and appealing, but lacking genuineness. They are often quick to form friendships, but once a relationship is established, can become egocentric and inconsiderate. They may constantly demand reassurance because of feelings of helplessness and dependency. Their actions are often inconsistent, and may be misinterpreted by others.

In relationships they attempt to control the opposite sex or to enter into a dependent relationship. Flights into romantic fantasy are common. The actual quality of their sexual relationships is variable. Some are promiscuous; others, naive and sexually unresponsive; and still others, apparently normal in their sexual adjustment.

Usually these people show little interest in intellectual achievement and careful, analytic thinking, but they are often creative and imaginative.

People with this disorder tend to be impressionable and easily influenced by others or by fads. They are apt to be overly trusting of others and suggestible, and to show an initially positive response to any strong authority figure who, they think, can provide a magical solution for their problems. Though they adopt convictions strongly and readily, their judgment is not firmly rooted, and they often play hunches.

Frequent complaints of poor health, such as weakness or headaches, or subjective feelings of depersonalization may be present. During periods of extreme stress, people with this disorder may experience transient psychotic symptoms, but they are generally of insufficient severity or duraton to warrant an additional diagnosis.

d. Narcissistic

1) *Essential Feature*

The essential feature of this disorder is a pervasive pattern of grandiosity (in fantasy or behavior), hypersensitivity to the evaluation of others, and lack of empathy that begins by early adulthood and is present in a variety of contexts.

People with this disorder have a grandiose sense of self-importance. They tend to exaggerate their accomplishments and talents, and expect to be noticed as "special" even without appropriate achievement. They often feel that because of their "specialness," their problems are unique, and can be understood only by other special people. Frequently this sense of self-importance alternates with feelings of special unworthiness. For example, a student who ordinarily expects an A and receives a grade of A minus may, at that moment, express the view that he or she is thus revealed to all as a failure. Conversely, having gotten an A, the student may feel fraudulent, and unable to take genuine pleasure in a real achievement.

These people are preoccupied with fantasies of unlimited success, power, brilliance, beauty, or ideal love, and with chronic feelings of envy for those whom they perceive as being more successful than they are. Although these fantasies frequently substitute for realistic activity, when such goals are actually pursued, it is often with a driven, pleasureless quality and an ambition that cannot be satisfied.

Self-esteem is almost invariably very fragile; the person may be preoccupied with how well he or she is doing and how well he or she is regarded by others. This often takes the form of an almost exhibitionistic need for constant attention and admiration. The person may constantly fish for compliments, often with great charm. In response to criticism, he or she may react with rage, shame, or humiliation, but mask these feelings with an aura of cool indifference.

Interpersonal relationships are invariably disturbed. A lack of empathy (inability to recognize and experience how others feel) is common. For example, the person may be unable to understand why a friend whose father has just died does not want to go to a party. A sense of entitlement, an unreasonable expectation of especially favorable treatment, is usually present. For example, such a person may assume that he or she does not have to wait in line when others must. Interpersonal exploitativeness, in which others are taken advantage of in order to achieve one's ends, or for self-aggrandizement, is common. Friendships are often made only after the person considers how he or she can profit from them. In romantic relationships, the partner is often treated as an object to be used to bolster the person's self-esteem.

2) *Associated Features*

Frequently, many of the features of Histrionic, Borderline, and Antisocial Personality Disorders are present; in some cases more than one diagnosis may be warranted.

Depressed mood is extremely common. Often the person is painfully self-conscious and preoccupied with grooming and remaining youthful. Personal deficits, defeats, or irresponsible behavior may be justified by rationalization or lying. Feelings may be faked in order to impress others.

3. Cluster C (Anxious or Fearful)

a. Avoidant

1) *Essential Feature*

The essential feature of this disorder is a pervasive pattern of social discomfort, fear of negative evaluation, and timidity, beginning by early adulthood and present in a variety of contexts.

Most people are somewhat concerned about how others assess them, but those with this disorder are easily hurt by criticism and are devastated by the slightest hint of disapproval. They generally are unwilling to enter into relationships unless given an unusually strong guarantee of uncritical acceptance; consequently, they often have no close friends or confidants (or only one) other than first-degree relatives.

Social or occupational activities that involve significant interpersonal contact tend to be avoided. For example, a promotion that will increase social demands may be avoided. In social situations, these people are reticent because of a fear of saying something inappropriate or foolish, or of being unable to answer a question. They fear being embarrassed by blushing, crying, or showing signs of anxiety before other people.

Generalized timidity produces resistance to doing anything that will deviate from the person's normal routine. Often the potential difficulties, physical dangers, or risks involved in doing something ordinary, but outside the person's usual activities, are exaggerated. For example, the person may cancel an important trip because of a remote possibility that heavy rain will make driving dangerous.

Unlike people with Schizoid Personality Disorder, who are socially isolated, but have no desire for social relations, those with Avoidant Personality Disorder yearn for affection and acceptance. They are distressed by their lack of ability to relate comfortably to others.

2) *Associated Features*

Depression, anxiety, and anger at oneself for failing to develop social relations are commonly experienced. Specific phobias may also be present.

b. Dependent

1) *Essential Feature*

The essential feature of this disorder is a pervasive pattern of dependent and submissive behavior beginning by early adulthood and present in a variety of contexts.

People with this disorder are unable to make everyday decisions without an excessive amount of advice and reassurance from others, and will even allow others to make most of their important decisions. For example, an adult with this disorder will typically assume a passive role and allow his or her spouse to decide where they should live, what kind of job he or she should have, and with which neighbors they should be friendly. A child or adolescent with this disorder may allow his or her parent(s) to decide what he or she should wear, with whom to associate, how to spend free time, and what school or college to attend.

This excessive dependence on others leads to difficulty in initiating projects or doing things on one's own. People with this disorder tend to feel uncomfortable or helpless when alone, and will go to great lengths to avoid being alone. They are devastated when close relationships end, and tend to be preoccupied with fears of being abandoned.

These people are easily hurt by criticism and disapproval, and tend to subordinate themselves to others, agreeing with people even when they believe them to be wrong, for fear of being rejected. They will volunteer to do things that are unpleasant or demeaning in order to get others to like them.

2) *Associated Features*

Frequently another Personality Disorder is present, such as Histrionic, Schizotypal, Narcissistic, or Avoidant Personality Disorder. Anxiety and depression are common.

People with this disorder invariably lack self-confidence. They tend to belittle their abilities and assets. For example, a person with this disorder may constantly refer to himself or herself as "stupid." They may at times seek, or stimulate, overprotection and dominance in others.

c. Obsessive Compulsive

  1) *Essential Feature*

The essential feature of this disorder is a pervasive pattern of perfectionism and inflexibility, beginning by early adulthood and present in a variety of contexts.

These people constantly strive for perfection, but this adherence to their own overly strict and often unattainable standards frequently interferes with actual completion of tasks and projects. No matter how good an accomplishment, it often does not seem "good enough." Preoccupation with rules, efficiency, trivial details, procedures, or form interferes with the ability to take a broad view of things. For example, such a person, having misplaced a list of things to be done, will spend an inordinate amount of time looking for the list rather than spend a few moments re-creating the list from memory and proceed with accomplishing the tasks. Time is poorly allocated, the most important tasks being left to the last moment.

People with this disorder are always mindful of their relative status in dominance-submission relationships. Although they resist the authority of others, they stubbornly and unreasonably insist that people conform to their way of doing things.

Work and productivity are prized to the exclusion of pleasure and interpersonal relationships. Often there is preoccupation with logic and intellect and intolerance of affective behavior in others. When pleasure is considered, it is something to be planned and worked for. However, the person usually keeps postponing the pleasurable activity, such as a vacation, so that it may never occur.

Decision making is avoided, postponed, or protracted, perhaps because of an inordinate fear of making a mistake. For example, assignments cannot be completed on time because the person is ruminating about priorities. This indecisiveness may cause the person to retain worn or worthless objects even when they have no sentimental value.

People with this disorder tend to be excessively conscientious, moralistic, scrupulous, and judgmental of self and others — for example, considering it "sinful" for a neighbor to leave her child's bicycle out in the rain.

People with this disorder are stingy with their emotions and material possessions. They tend not to express their feelings, and rarely give compliments or gifts. Everyday relationships have a conventional, formal, and serious quality. Others often perceive these people as stilted or "stiff."

2) *Associated Features*

People with this disorder may complain of difficulty expressing tender feelings. They may experience considerable distress because of their indecisiveness and general ineffectiveness. Their speech may be circumstantial. Depressed mood is common. These people have an unusually strong need to be in control. When they are unable to control others, a situation, or their environment, they often ruminate about the situation and become angry, although the anger is usually not expressed directly. (For example, a man may be angry when service in a restaurant is poor, but instead of complaining to the management, ruminates about how much he will leave as a tip.) Frequently there is extreme sensitivity to social criticism, especially if it comes from someone with considerable status or authority.

d. Passive Aggressive

1) *Essential Feature*

The essential feature of this disorder is a pervasive pattern of passive resistance to demands for adequate social and occupational performance, beginning by early adulthood and present in a variety of contexts. The resistance is expressed indirectly rather than directly, and results in pervasive and persistent social and occupational ineffectiveness even when more self-assertive and effective behavior is possible. The name of this disorder is based on the assumption that such people are passively expressing covert aggression.

People with this disorder habitually resent and oppose demands to increase or maintain a given level of functioning. This occurs most clearly in work situations, but is also evident in social functioning. The resistance is expressed indirectly through such maneuvers as procrastination, dawdling, stubbornness, intentional inefficiency, and "forgetfulness." These people obstruct the efforts of others by failing to do their share of the work. For example, when an executive gives a subordinate some material to review for a meeting the next morning, rather than complain that he has no time to do the work, the subordinate may misplace or misfile the

the material and thus attain his goal by passively resisting the demand on him.

These people become sulky, irritable, or argumentative when asked to do something they do not want to do. They often protest to others about how unreasonable the demands being made on them are, and resent useful suggestions from others concerning how to be more productive. As a result of their resentment of demands, they unreasonably criticize or scorn the people in authority who are making the demands.

2) *Associated Features*

Often people with this disorder are dependent and lack self-confidence. Typically, they are pessimistic about the future, but have no realization that their behavior is responsible for their difficulties.

It should be noted, finally, that oftentimes a diagnosis of *Personality Disorder not Otherwise Specified* (NOS) is made. This designation should be used, according to DSM III R, to refer to Disorders of personality functioning that are not classifiable as a specific Personality Disorder. A person, for example, may have features of more than one specific Personality Disorder that do not meet the full criteria of any one, yet cause significant impairment in social or occupational functioning, or subjective distress. Used in this sense, the Personality Disorder NOS was formerly referred to as a Mixed Personality Disorder.

This category, however, can also be used when the clinician judges that a specific Personality Disorder not included in this classification is appropriate, such as Impulsive Personality Disorder, Immature Personality Disorder, Self-defeating Personality Disorder or Sadistic Personality Disorder.

C. A Jurisprudence

As for the effect a Personality Disorder might have on the validity of a marriage, the following remarks, grouped according to the four standard areas of investigation in cases of incompetence would seem in order.

1. *Severity*

The nature and degree of impairment resulting from Personality Disorders depends on the type and severity of the Disorder in question. In every case, therefore, the judge must determine whether or not the disorder has, in fact, rendered the person incompetent, i.e. disabled from assuming the essential obligations of marriage.

2. *Antecedence*

Whenever a Personality Disorder has been diagnosed, it may be presumed to have antedated the marriage, since Personality Disorders are, usually from adolescence, part of the warp and woof of the personality.

3. *Perpetuity*

Usually a severe Personality Disorder will result in disruptive behavior early on in a marriage, making it clear that the person lacked the ability at the time of marriage to assume the essential obligations. In those cases, however, where the couple truly relate well for the first several years of marriage, the judge must consider the possibility that the disorder was moderate and controllable at the time of marriage and was not therefore invalidating. In order to arrive at a decision in a case of this sort it will be particularly helpful to have a complete anamnesis of the person, describing the person's premarital (including pre-adolescent and adolescent) as well as postmarital behavior.

4. *Relativity*

It is also possible in a given marriage that the two people both suffer from moderate disorders not sufficiently severe to render them absolutely incompetent as individuals but so conflicting that the two people are incompetent relative to each other. For example, two people who suffer from moderate Dependent Personality Disorders marry each other. They are both in need of a supportive, nurturant person as a spouse but are unable to meet each other's needs and the marriage flounders from the beginning. A judge may justifiably conclude that the couple, as a couple, was incompetent for marriage, or, perhaps more accurately (from a jurisprudential point of view), that one party was incompetent for marriage with the other.

ANXIETY DISORDERS

A. Description

Anxiety Disorders are a group of disorders involving symptoms of anxiety and avoidance behavior.

In terms of their being potentially disruptive of a marital relationship, the most notable Anxiety Disorders are Agoraphobia, Obsessive Compulsive Disorder and Post-traumatic Stress Disorder. These are described in DSM III R as follows:

B. Agoraphobia

Agoraphobia is the fear of being in places or situations from which escape might be difficult (or embarrassing), or in which help might not be available in the event of suddenly developing a symptom(s) that could be incapacitating or extremely embarrassing. As a result of this fear, the person either restricts travel or needs a companion when away from home, or else endures agoraphobic situations despite intense anxiety. Common agoraphobic situations include being outside the home alone, being in a crowd or standing in a line, being on a bridge, and traveling in a bus, train, or car.

Usually the person is afraid of having a *limited symptom attack,* that is, developing a single or small number of symptoms, such as becoming dizzy or falling, depersonalization or derealization, loss of bladder or bowel control, vomiting, or having cardiac distress. In some of these cases, such symptoms have occurred in the past, and the person may be preoccupied with fears of their recurrence. In other cases, the person has never experienced the symptom(s), but nevertheless fears that the symptom "could" develop and incapacitate him or her or be extremely embarrassing. In a small number of cases the person fears feeling incapacitated in some way, but is unable to specify what symptom he or she fears.

C. Obsessive Compulsive Disorder

1. *Essential Feature*

   The essential feature of this disorder is recurrent obsessions or compulsions sufficiently severe to cause marked distress, be time-consuming, or significantly interfere with the person's normal routine, occupational functioning, or usual social activities or relationships with others.

   Obsessions are persistent ideas, thoughts, impulses, or images that are experienced, at least initially, as intrusive and senseless—for example, a parent having repeated impulses to kill a loved child, or a religious person having recurrent blasphemous thoughts. The person attempts to ignore or suppress such thoughts or impulses or to neutralize them with some other thought or action. The person recognizes that the obsessions are the product of his or her own mind, and are not imposed from without (as in the delusion of thought insertion).

The most common obsessions are repetitive thoughts of violence (e.g., killing one's child), contamination (e.g., becoming infected by shaking hands), and doubt (e.g., repeatedly wondering whether one has performed some act, such as having hurt someone in a traffic accident).

Compulsions are repetitive, purposeful, and intentional behaviors that are performed in response to an obsession, according to certain rules, or in a stereotyped fashion. The behavior is designed to neutralize or to prevent discomfort or some dreaded event or situation. However, either the activity is not connected in a realistic way with what it is designed to neutralize or prevent, or it is clearly excessive. The act is performed with a sense of subjective compulsion that is coupled with a desire to resist the compulsion (at least initially). The person recognizes that his or her behavior is excessive or unreasonable (this may not be true for young children and may no longer be true for people whose obsessions have evolved into overvalued ideas) and does not derive pleasure from carrying out the activity, although it provides a release of tension. The most common compulsions involve hand-washing, counting, checking, and touching.

When the person attempts to resist a compulsion, there is a sense of mounting tension that can be immediately relieved by yielding to the compulsion. In the course of the illness, after repeated failure at resisting the compulsions, the person may give in to them and no longer experience a desire to resist them.

2. *Associated Features*

Depression and anxiety are common. Frequently there is phobic avoidance of situations that involve the content of the obsessions, such as dirt or contamination. For example, a person with obsessions about dirt may avoid public restrooms; a person with obsessions about contamination may avoid shaking hands with strangers.

D. Post-Traumatic Stress Disorder

1. *Essential Feature*

The essential feature of this disorder is the development of characteristic symptoms following a psychologically distressing event that is outside the range of usual human experience (i.e., outside the range of such common experiences as simple bereavement, chronic illness, business losses, and marital conflict). The stressor producing this syndrome would be markedly distressing to almost anyone, and is usually experienced with intense fear, terror, and helplessness. The characteristic symptoms involve reexperiencing the traumatic event, avoidance of stimuli associated with the event or numbing of general responsiveness, and increased arousal. The diagnosis is not made if the disturbance lasts less than one month.

The most common traumata involve either a serious threat to one's life or physical integrity; a serious threat or harm to one's children, spouse, or other close relatives and friends; sudden destruction of one's home or community; or seeing another person who has recently been, or is being, seriously injured or killed as the result of an accident or physical violence. In some cases the trauma may be learning about a serious threat or harm to a close friend or relative, e.g., that one's child has been kidnapped, tortured, or killed.

The trauma may be experienced alone (e.g., rape or assault) or in the company of groups of people (e.g., military combat). Stressors producing this disorder include natural disasters (e.g., floods, earthquakes), accidental disasters (e.g., car accidents with serious physical injury, airplane crashes, large fires, collapse of physical structures), or deliberately caused disasters (e.g., bombing, torture, death camps). Some stressors frequently produce the disorder (e.g., torture), and others produce it only occasionally (e.g., natural disasters or car accidents). Sometimes there is a concomitant physical component of the trauma, which may even involve direct damage to the central nervous system (e.g., malnutrition, head injury). The disorder is apparently more severe and longer lasting when the stressor is of human design.

The traumatic event can be reexperienced in a variety of ways. Commonly the person has recurrent and intrusive recollections of the event or recurrent distressing dreams during which the event is reexperienced. In rare instances there are dissociative states, lasting from a few seconds to several hours, or even days, during which components of the event are relived, and the person behaves as though experiencing the event at that moment. There is often intense psychological distress when the person is exposed to events that resemble an aspect of the traumatic event or that symbolize the traumatic event, such as anniversaries of the event.

In addition to the reexperiencing of the trauma, there is persistent avoidance of stimuli associated with it, or a numbing of general responsiveness that was not present before the trauma. The person commonly makes deliberate efforts to avoid thoughts or feelings about the traumatic event and about activities or situations that arouse recollections of it. This avoidance of reminders of the trauma may include psychogenic amnesia for an important aspect of the traumatic event.

Diminished responsiveness to the external world, referred to as "psychic numbing" or "emotional anesthesia," usually begins soon after the traumatic event. A person may complain of feeling detached or estranged from other people, that he or she has lost the ability to become interested in previously enjoyed activities, or that the ability to feel emotions of any type, especially those associated with intimacy, tenderness, and sexuality, is markedly decreased.

Persistent symptoms of increased arousal that were not present before the trauma include difficulty falling or staying asleep (recurrent nightmares during which the traumatic event is relived are sometimes accompanied by middle or terminal sleep disturbance), hypervigilance, and exaggerated startle response. Some complain of difficulty in concentrating or in completing tasks. Many report changes in aggression. In mild cases this may take the form of irritability with fears of losing control. In more severe forms, particularly in cases in which the survivor has actually committed acts of violence (as in war veterans), the fear is conscious and pervasive, and the reduced capacity for modulation may express itself in unpredictable explosions of aggressive behavior or an inability to express angry feelings.

Symptoms characteristic of Post-traumatic Stress Disorder, or physiologic reactivity, are often intensified or precipitated when the person is exposed to situations or activities that resemble or symbolize the original trauma (e.g., cold snowy weather or uniformed guards for survivors of death camps in cold climates; hot, humid weather for veterans of the South Pacific).

2.   *Associated Features*

Symptoms of depression and anxiety are common, and in some instances may be sufficiently severe to be diagnosed as an Anxiety or Depressive Disorder. Impulsive behavior can occur, such as suddenly changing place of residence, unexplained absences, or other changes in life-style. There may be symptoms of an Organic Mental Disorder, such as failing memory, difficulty in concentrating, emotional lability, headache, and vertigo. In the case of a life-threatening trauma shared with others, survivors often describe painful guilt feelings about surviving when others did not, or about the things they had to do in order to survive.

E.   A Jurisprudence

When the four usual areas of investigation are applied to the Anxiety Disorders, the following observations might be useful.

1.   *Severity*

DSM III R notes that in the case of *Agoraphobia* impairment is usually severe; that in the case of the *Obsessive Compulsive Disorder* it is often moderate or severe and, in some cases, acting according to the compulsions may become the major life activity; and that in the case of *Post-traumatic Stress Disorder* impairment may often be severe and affect nearly every aspect of life. DSM III R goes on to note that in the case of Post-traumatic Stress Disorder, phobic avoidance of situations or activities resembling or symbolizing the original trauma may interfere with interpersonal relationships such

66

as marriage or family life. Emotional lability, depression, and guilt may result in self-defeating behavior or suicidal actions.

When sufficiently severe, therefore, these disorders clearly have the potential for depriving the person of the capacity for self revelation, understanding and loving.

2. *Antecedence*

In order to determine whether the disorder was present at the time of the exchange of consent the court must examine the behavior of the person prior to and immediately following the wedding.

3. *Perpetuity*

If the disorder was present at the time of the wedding and if it eventually destroyed the marriage because the affected person was unable to fulfill the essential obligations of marriage, especially self revelation, understanding and loving, then the person must be considered to have lacked due competence for the marriage since he or she was not, at the time of the wedding, able to assume the perpetual obligations of marriage.

4. *Relativity*

The low threshold of the other spouse to relate to even a moderately impaired partner could, in practice, result in relative incompetence.

SCHIZOPHRENIA

A. Description

Schizophrenia is a psychosis (that is, a disorder in which impairment of mental function has developed to a degree that interferes grossly with insight, ability to meet some ordinary demands of life or to maintain adequate contact with reality) that involves delusions, hallucinations or certain characteristic disturbances in affect and the form of thought.

B. Characteristic Disturbances

1. *Content of thought.* The major disturbance in the content of thought involves delusions that are often multiple, fragmented, or bizarre (i.e., involving a phenomenon that in the person's culture would be regarded as totally implausible, e.g., thought broadcasting, or being controlled by a dead person). Simple persecutory delusions involving the belief that others are spying on, spreading false rumors about, or planning to harm the person are common. Delusions of reference, in which events, objects, or other people are given particular and unusual significance, usually of a negative or pejorative nature, are also common. For example, the person may be convinced that a television commentator is mocking him.

   Certain delusions are observed far more frequently in Schizophrenia than in other psychotic disorders. These include, for instance, the belief or experience that one's thoughts, as they occur, are broadcast from one's head to the external world so that others can hear them (thought broadcasting); that thoughts that are not one's own are inserted into one's mind (thought insertion); that thoughts have been removed from one's head (thought withdrawal); or that one's feelings, impulses, thoughts, or actions are not one's own, but are imposed by some external force (delusions of being controlled). Less commonly, somatic, grandiose, religious, and nihilistic delusions are observed.

2. *Form of thought.* A disturbance in the form of thought is often present. This has been referred to as "formal thought disorder," and is different from a disorder in the content of thought. The most common example of this is loosening of associations, in which ideas shift from one subject to another, completely unrelated or only obliquely related subject, without the speaker's displaying any awareness that the topics are unconnected. Statements that lack a meaningful relationship may be juxtaposed, or the person may shift idiosyncratically from one frame of reference to another. When loosening of associations is severe, the person may become incoherent, that is, his or her speech may become incomprehensible.

   There may be poverty of content of speech, in which speech is adequate in amount, but conveys little information because it is vague, overly abstract, or overly concrete, repetitive, or stereotyped. The listener can recognize this disturbance by noting that little if any information has been conveyed although the person has spoken at some length. Less common disturbances include neologisms, perseveration, clanging, and blocking.

3. *Perception.* The major disturbances in perception are various forms of hallucinations. Although these occur in all modalities, the most common are auditory hallucinations, which frequently involve many voices the person perceives as coming from outside his or her head. The voices may be familiar, and often make insulting remarks; they may be single or multiple. Voices speaking directly to the person or commenting on his or her ongoing behavior are particularly characteristic. Command hallucinations may be obeyed, which sometimes creates danger for the person or others. Occasionally, the auditory hallucinations are of sounds rather than voices.

   Tactile hallucinations may be present, and typically involve electrical, tingling, or burning sensations. Somatic hallucinations, such as the sensation of snakes crawling inside the abdomen, are occasionally experienced. Visual, gustatory, and olfactory hallucinations also occur, but with less frequency, and, in the absence of auditory hallucinations, always raise the possibility of an Organic Mental Disorder. Other perceptual abnormalities include sensations of bodily change; hypersensitivity to sound, sight, and smell; illusions; and synethesias.

4. *Affect.* The disturbance often involves flat or inappropriate affect. In flat affect, there are virtually no signs of affective expression; the voice is usually monotonous and the face, immobile. The person may complain that he or she no longer responds with normal emotional intensity or, in extreme cases, no longer has feelings.In inappropriate affect, the affect is clearly discordant with the content of the person's speech or ideation. For example, while discussing being tortured by electrical shocks, a person with Schizophrenia, Disorganized Type, may laugh or smile. Sudden and unpredictable changes in affect involving inexplicable outbursts of anger may occur.

   Although these affective disturbances are almost invariably part of the clinical picture, their presence is often difficult to detect except when they are in an extreme form. Furthermore, antipsychotic drugs have effects that may appear similar to the affective flattening seen in Schizophrenia.

5. *Sense of self.* The sense of self that gives the normal person a feeling of individuality, uniqueness, and self-direction is frequently disturbed in Schizophrenia. This is sometimes referred to as a loss of ego boundaries, and frequently is evidenced by extreme perplexity about one's own identity and the meaning of existence, or by some of the specific delusions described above, particularly those involving control by an outside force.

6. *Volition.* The characteristic disturbances in volition are most readily observed in the residual phase. There is nearly always some disturbance in self-initiated, goal-directed activity, which may grossly impair work or other

role functioning. This may take the form of inadequate interest, drive, or ability to follow a course of action to its logical conclusion. Marked ambivalence regarding alternative courses of action can lead to near-cessation of goal-directed activity.

7. *Impaired interpersonal functioning and relationship to the external world.* Difficulty in interpersonal relationships is almost invariably present. Often this takes the form of social withdrawal and emotional detachment. When the person is severely preoccupied with egocentric and illogical ideas and fantasies and distorts or excludes the external world, the condition has been referred to as "autism." Some with the disorder, during a phase of the illness, cling to other people, intrude upon strangers, and fail to recognize that excessive closeness makes other people uncomfortable and likely to pull away.

8. *Psychomotor behavior.* Various disturbances in psychomotor behavior are observed, particularly in the chronically severe and acutely florid forms of the disorder. There may be a marked decrease in reactivity to the environment, with a reduction in spontaneous movements and activity. In extreme cases the person appears unaware of the nature of the environ-ment (as in catatonic stupor); may maintain a rigid posture and resist efforts to be moved (as in catatonic rigidity); may make apparently purposeless and stereotyped, excited motor movements not influenced by external stimuli (as in catatonic excitement); may voluntarily assume inappropriate or bizarre postures (as in catatonic posturing); or may resist and actively counteract instructions or attempts to be moved (as in catatonic nega-tivism). In addition, odd mannerisms, grimacing, or waxy flexibility may be present.

C. A Jurisprudence

1. The typical scenario involving a schizophrenic that comes to the attention of a Tribunal includes a fairly youthful marriage prior to the first psychotic episode; then one or more, often extended, hospitalizations; the deteriora-tion of the schizophrenic spouse; and the termination of any genuine relationship between husband and wife.

2. As in all cases involving lack of due competence, it is important for the Court to examine the four usual areas. As applied to the Schizophrenic Disorders, the following observations may be made:

a. *Severity*

Schizophrenia is grossly disabling and is characterized generally as a loss of contact with the real world.

b. *Antecedence*

Whenever the schizophrenia of one of the spouses destroys the marriage, the antecedence of the incompetence can usually be demonstrated. Generally the prepsychotic personality of the person who later develops a schizophrenic disorder is itself pathological. Often the person is shy, withdrawn and schizoid, without close friends and sometimes antisocial early on in life. Also, the onset of these disorders is insidious and subtle, with a prodromal or precursive period during which social withdrawal, diminished effectiveness at school or work, depression and anxiety are in evidence. The Court should investigate the psychological state of the person at the time of marriage, but once there is evidence that the proximate disposition for what later became a full blown disorder was indeed present at the time of marriage, it may be fairly concluded that the incompetence was at least virtually and causally antecedent to the marriage.

c. *Perpetuity*

If a schizophrenic disorder does, in fact, eventually render a spouse incapable of *fulfilling* the essential obligations of marriage then, since marital obligations are, by their nature, perpetual, a tribunal is justified, assuming that a proximate disposition for the disorder can be shown to have existed at the time of the wedding, in concluding that, at the time of the marriage, the person was incapable of *assuming* those obligations.

d. *Relativity*

Given the pervasiveness of this disorder, the relativity of the incompetence is not really a factor.

MOOD DISORDERS

A. Description

Mood Disorders are disorders that involve a disturbance of mood accompanied by a full or partial Manic or Depressive Syndrome that is not due to any other physical or mental disorder. Mood refers to a prolonged emotion that colors the whole psychic life; it generally involves either depression or elation.

B. Types

Mood Disorders are of two types: *Bipolar Disorders* (involving one or more Manic or Hypomanic Episodes, usually with a history of Major Depressive Episodes) and *Depressive Disorders* (involving one or more periods of depression without a history of either Manic or Hypomanic Episodes).

C. Description Of Episodes

1. *Manic Episode*
   The essential feature of a Manic Episode is a distinct period during which the predominant mood is either elevated, expansive, or irritable, and there are associated symptoms of the Manic Syndrome. The disturbance is sufficiently severe to cause marked impairment in occupational functioning or in usual social activities or relationships with others, or to require hospitalization to prevent harm to self or others. The associated symptoms include inflated self-esteem or grandiosity (which may be delusional), decreased need for sleep, pressure of speech, flight of ideas, distractibility, increased involvement in goal-directed activity, psychomotor agitation, and excessive involvement in pleasurable activities which have a high potential for painful consequences that the person often does not recognize. The diagnosis is made only if it cannot be established that an organic factor initiated and maintained the disturbance. In addition, the diagnosis is not made if the disturbance is superimposed on Schizophrenia, Schizophreniform Disorder, Delusional Disorder, or Psychotic Disorder NOS, or if the criteria for Schizoaffective Disorder are met.

   The elevated mood may be described as euphoric, unusually good, cheerful, or high, often having an infectious quality for the uninvolved observer, but recognized as excessive by those who know the person well. The expansive quality of the mood disturbance is characterized by unceasing and unselective enthusiasm for interacting with people and seeking involvement with other aspects of the environment. Although elevated mood is considered the prototypic symptom, the predominant mood disturbance may be irritability, which may be most apparent when the person is thwarted.

   Characteristically, there is inflated self-esteem, ranging from uncritical self-confidence to marked grandiosity, which may be delusional. For instance, the person may give advice on matters about which he or she has no special knowledge, such as how to run a mental hospital or the United Nations. Despite lack of any particular talent, the person may start a novel, compose music, or seek publicity for some impractical invention. Grandiose delusions involving a special relationship to God or some well-known figure from the political, religious, or entertainment world are common.

Almost invariably there is a decreased need for sleep; the person awakens several hours before the usual time, full of energy. When the sleep disturbance is severe, the person may go for days without any sleep at all, yet not feel tired.

Manic speech is typically loud, rapid, and difficult to interrupt. Often it is full of jokes, puns, plays on words, and amusing irrelevancies. It may become theatrical, with dramatic mannerisms and singing. Sounds rather than meaningful conceptual relationships may govern word choice (clanging). If the person's mood is more irritable than expansive, his or her speech may be marked by complaints, hostile comments, and angry tirades.

Frequently there is flight of ideas, i.e., a nearly continuous flow of accelerated speech, with abrupt changes from topic to topic, usually based on understandable associations, distracting stimuli, or plays on words. When flight of ideas is severe, speech may be disorganized and incoherent. However, loosening of associations and incoherence may occur even when there is no flight of ideas, particularly if the person is on medication.

Distractibility is usually present, and is evidenced by rapid changes in speech or activity as a result of responding to various irrelevant external stimuli, such as background noise, or signs or pictures on the wall.

The increase in goal-directed activity often involves excessive planning of, and participation in, multiple activities (e.g., sexual, occupational, political, religious). Almost invariably there is increased sociability, which includes efforts to renew old acquaintanceships and calling friends at all hours of the night. The person does not recognize the intrusive, domineering, and demanding nature of these interactions. Frequently, expansiveness, un-warranted optimism, grandiosity, and lack of judgment lead to such activities as buying sprees, reckless driving, foolish business investments, and sexual behavior unusual for the person. Often the activities have a disorganized, flamboyant, or bizarre quality, for example, dressing in colorful or strange garments, wearing excessive, poorly applied makeup, or distributing candy, money, or advice to passing strangers.

2. *Major Depressive Episode*

The essential feature of a Major Depressive Episode is either depressed mood (or possibly, in children or adolescents, an irritable mood) or loss of interest or pleasure in all, or almost all, activities, and associated symptoms, for a period of at least two weeks. The symptoms represent a change from previous functioning and are relatively persistent, that is, they occur for most of the day, nearly every day, during at least a two-week period. The associated symptoms include appetite disturbance, change in weight, sleep disturbance, psychomotor agitation or retardation, decreased energy, feelings of worthlessness or excessive or inappropriate guilt, difficulty thinking or concentrating, and recurrent thoughts of death, or suicidal ideation or attempts. The diagnosis is made only if it cannot be established that an organic factor initiated and maintained the disturbance and the disturbance is not the normal reaction to the loss of a loved one (Uncomplicated Bereavement). In addition, the diagnosis is not made if the disturbance is superimposed on Schizophrenia, Schizophreniform Disorder, Delusional Disorder, or Psychotic Disorder NOS, or if the criteria for Schizoaffective Disorder are met.

A person with depressed mood will usually describe feeling depressed, sad, hopeless, discouraged, "down in the dumps," or some other colloquial equivalent. In some cases, although the person may deny feeling depressed, the presence of depressed mood can be inferred from others' observing that the person looks sad or depressed.

Loss of interest or pleasure is probably always present in a Major Depressive Episode to some degree, and is often described by the person as not being as interested in usual activities as previously, "not caring anymore," or, more rarely, a painful inability to experience pleasure. The person may not complain of loss of interest or pleasure, but family members generally will notice withdrawal from friends and family and neglect of avocations that were previously a source of pleasure.

Appetite is frequently disturbed, loss of appetite being the more common, but increased appetite sometimes being evident. When loss of appetite is severe, there may be significant weight loss or, in the case of children, failure to make expected weight gains. When appetite is markedly increased, there may be significant weight gain.

Sleep is commonly disturbed, the more frequent complaint being insomnia, but sometimes hypersomnia. The insomnia may involve difficulty falling asleep (initial insomnia), waking up during sleep and then returning to sleep only with difficulty (middle insomnia), or early morning awakening (terminal insomnia). Hypersomnia may involve sleeping for a longer period of time than is usual, daytime sleepiness, or taking excessive naps. Sometimes the sleep disturbance, rather than the depressed mood or loss of interest or pleasure, is the main symptom that brings the person into treatment.

Psychomotor agitation takes the form of inability to sit still, pacing, hand-wringing, pulling or rubbing of hair, skin, clothing, or other objects. Psychomotor retardation may takes the form of slowed speech, increased pauses before answering, soft or monotonous speech, slowed body movements, a markedly decreased amount of speech (poverty of speech), or muteness. A decrease in energy level is almost invariably present, and is experienced as sustained fatigue even in the absence of physical exertion. The smallest task may seem difficult or impossible to accomplish.

The sense of worthlessness varies from feelings of inadequacy to completely unrealistic negative evaluations of one's worth. The person may reproach himself or herself for minor failings that are exaggerated and search the environment for cues confirming the negative self-evaluation. Guilt may be expressed as an excessive reaction to either current or past failings or as exaggerated responsibility for some untoward or tragic event. The sense of worthlessness or guilt may be of delusional proportions.

Difficulty in concentrating, slowed thinking, and indecisiveness are frequent. The person may complain of memory difficulty and appear easily distracted.

Thoughts of death (not just fear of dying) are common. Often there is the belief that the person or others would be better off dead. There may be suicidal thoughts, with or without a specific plan, or suicide attempts.

D. Course Of Episodes

1. *Manic* episodes typically begin suddenly with a rapid escalation of symptoms over a few days. The episodes usually last from a few days to months and are briefer and end more abruptly than Major Depressive Episodes.

2. The onset of a *Major Depressive* Episode is variable, the syptoms usually developing over days to weeks; in some cases, however, it may be sudden (e.g., when associated with severe psychosocial stress). In some instances prodromal symptoms—e.g., generalized anxiety, panic attacks, phobias, or mild depressive symptoms—may occur over a period of several months.

    The duration of a Major Depressive Episode is also variable. Untreated, the episode typically lasts six months or longer. Usually there is a complete remission of symptoms, and general functioning returns to the premorbid level; but in a large proportion of cases, some symptoms of the episode persist for as long as two years without a period of two months or longer without significant depressive symptoms.

E. A Jurisprudence

1. Marriage cases involving a person with a major mood disorder are fairly uncommon these days but occasionally it will happen that the marriage will occur before the first episode, or perhaps between episodes, and that after marriage the episodes will be so frequent and severe that they are disruptive of marital life.

2. In making a judgment on validity, all four of the standard areas of investigation regarding incompetence must be considered.

    a. *Severity*

        In manic episodes there is usually considerable impairment in both social and occupational functioning and a need for protection from the consequences of poor judgment or hyperactivity.

        In major depressive episodes the degree of impairment varies, but there is always some interference in social and occupational functioning. If impairment is severe, the individual may be totally unable to function socially or occupationally, or even to feed or clothe himself or herself or maintain minimal personal hygiene.

        In between episodes the person may function fairly normally but the episodes themselves may easily be destructive of a marriage.

    b. *Antecedence*

        The precise etiology of the Mood Disorders is not clear. Perhaps hereditary, constitutional, biological and psychological factors all play a part. It seems clear, however, that some kind of predisposition for the severe disorder certainly exists. Therefore, even when the first episode occurs after marriage, antecedence may be presumed.

    c. *Perpetuity*

        Oftentimes a Mood Disorder can be controlled by the use of chemotherapy. Such therapy, if successful, can prevent florid episodic manic attacks and often episodic depressions. Though the chemotherapy may have to be continued indefinitely, when successful, a relatively normal life is possible. Relative to the marriage, however, it is still possible that such a disorder would destroy the marriage before it could be controlled. In such a case the person lacked due competence for marriage since, at the time of the wedding, he or she was not capable of assuming the *perpetual* obligations of marriage.

    d. *Relativity*

        It may be that, in the case at bar, the "other party," usually the petitioner, is a walking precipitating factor for the respondent's disorder. Should this be true, it is possible that the respondent could function in another marriage but not in the marriage under consideration.

ALCOHOL DEPENDENCE

A. Essential Feature

The essential feature of Alcohol Dependence is a cluster of cognitive, behavioral and physiologic symptoms that indicate that the person has impaired control of alcohol and continues to use it despite adverse consequences.

B. Symptoms of Dependence

DSM III R lists the following nine symptoms of dependence on psychoactive substances in general, including, of course, alcohol. For a diagnosis of Dependence at least three of these symptoms must be present.

1. The person finds that when he or she actually takes the psychoactive substance, it is often in larger amounts or over a longer period than originally intended. For example, the person may decide to take only one drink of alcohol, but after taking this first drink, continues to drink until severely intoxicated.

2. The person recognizes that the substance use is excessive, and has attempted to reduce or control it, but has been unable to do so (as long as the substance is available). In other instances the person may want to reduce or control his or her substance use, but has never actually made an effort to do so.

3. A great deal of time is spent in activities necessary to procure the substance (including theft), taking it, or recovering from its effects. In mild cases the person may spend several hours a day taking the substance, but continue to be involved in other activities. In severe cases, virtually all of the user's daily activities revolve around obtaining, using, and recuperating from the effects of the substance.

4. The person may suffer intoxication or withdrawal symptoms when he or she is expected to fulfill major role obligations (work, school, homemaking). For example, the person may be intoxicated when working outside the home or when expected to take care of his or her children. In addition, the person may be intoxicated or have withdrawal symptoms in situations in which substance use is physically hazardous, such as driving a car or operating machinery.

5. Important social, occupational, or recreational activities are given up or reduced because of substance use. The person may withdraw from family activities and hobbies in order to spend more time with substance-using friends, or to use the substance in private.

6. With heavy and prolonged substance use, a variety of social, psychological, and physical problems occur, and are exacerbated by continued use of the substance. Despite having one or more of these problems (and recognizing that use of the substance causes or exacerbates them), the person continues to use the substance.

7.   Significant tolerance, a markedly diminished effect with continued use of the same amount of the substance, occurs. The person will then take greatly increased amounts of the substance in order to achieve intoxication or the desired effect. This is distinguished from the marked personal differences in initial sensitivity to the effects of a particular substance.

The degree to which tolerance develops varies greatly across classes of substances. Many cigarette-smokers consume more than 20 cigarettes a day, an amount that would have produced definite symptoms of toxicity when they first started smoking. Many heavy users of cannabis are not aware of tolerance to it, although tolerance has been demonstrated in some people. Whether there is tolerance to phencyclidine (PCP) and related substances is unclear. Heavy users of alcohol at the peak of their tolerance can consume only about 50% more than they originally needed in order to experience the effects of intoxication. In contrast, heavy users of opioids often increase the amount of opioids consumed to tenfold the amount they originally used—an amount that would be lethal to a nonuser. When the psychoactive substance used is illegal and perhaps mixed with various diluents or with other substances, tolerance may be difficult to determine.

8.   With continued use, characteristic withdrawal symptoms develop when the person stops or reduces intake of the substance. The withdrawal symptoms vary greatly across classes of substances. Marked and generally easily measured physiologic signs of withdrawal are common with alcohol, opioids, sedatives, hypnotics, and anxiolytics. Such signs are less obvious with amphetamines, cocaine, nicotine, and cannabis, but intense subjective symptoms can occur upon withrawal from heavy use of these substances. No significant withdrawal is seen even after repeated use of hallucinogens; withdrawal from PCP and related substances has not yet been described in humans, although it has been demonstrated in animals.

9.   After developing unpleasant withdrawal symptoms, the person begins taking the substance in order to relieve or avoid those symptoms. This typically involves using the substance throughout the day, beginning soon after awakening. This symptom is generally not present with cannabis, hallucinogens, and PCP.

C.   A Jurisprudence

1.   Marriage cases in which Alcohol Dependence is the only diagnosis are rare. Generally the psychiatric expert sees the alcoholism as one aspect of a larger syndrome. Occasionally, however, the drinking is so heavy and frequent, that there is no clear picture of how the person functions when sober, so that a broader diagnosis would not be justified by the evidence.

2.   In determining whether Alcohol Dependence is invalidating of a marriage, the usual four areas must be investigated.

a. *Severity*

Alcohol Dependence is profoundly disruptive of marriage life. Members of an alcoholic's family often live in fear, embarrassment and deprivation. And, almost by definition, the alcoholic lacks the capacity for those specifically marital acts of self revelation, understanding and loving; he is too self centered or bottle centered for that.

b. *Antecedence*

Generally, in cases that come before a tribunal, the alcoholic party was either already drinking excessively during the courtship but the other party did not consider it a serious problem, or the alcoholic had a drinking problem earlier in life but had managed to bring it under control prior to the marriage only to have it flare up again afterwards. In such cases it may be presumed that the incompetence resulting from the alcoholism was at least causally antecedent.

Occasionally the person whose Alcohol Dependence eventually destroys the marriage never drank at all before marriage. In such cases a rule of thumb might be that if alcohol abuse began in the first few years of marriage then the incompetence may be presumed to have been virtually antecedent, i.e. the proximate disposition to alcoholism and the proximate causes of its onset were present at the time of marriage. If, however, alcohol abuse began only after several years of marriage, then the legal presumption would be against antecedence.

c. *Perpetuity*

Since the essential obligations of marriage are perpetual obligations, a person must, in order to enter a valid marriage, have the capacity, at the time of the exchange of consent, to assume those perpetual obligations. If therefore it is shown 1) that a person suffered at least virtually or causally from Alcohol Dependence at the time of marriage and 2) that the cumulative effect of the drinking eventually deprived the person of the ability to fulfill the essential marital obligations, then the person is considered to have lacked due competence.

d. *Relativity*

The alcoholic's choice of partner could conceivably be critical. It could happen, for example, that a man who was abusing alcohol at the time of marriage but was not dependent on it, married a woman whose own problems would certainly exacerbate the man's attachment to alcohol. In such a case it could be argued that the alcohol abuse plus the exacerbating spouse would constitute marital incompetence, i.e. the incapacity of the man to function in marriage (that is, to fulfill perpetually the essential obligations of marriage) with this particular woman.

D. Similar Disorders

Other Psychoactive Substance Use Disorders, like Cannabis Dependence, Cocaine Dependence and Opioid Dependence, as well as certain Impulse Control Disorders like Kleptomania and Pathological Gambling would follow the same general jurisprudence outlined here.

HOMOSEXUALITY

A. Descriptiion

Homosexuality is a strong preferential erotic attraction to members of one's own sex.

DSM III R (see Index and DSM III p. 28) does not regard homosexuality in itself as a disorder. It is considered a disorder only when it is ego-dystonic, that is to say, in the case of a person for whom changing sexual orientation is a persistent concern.

Within the context of marital jurisprudence, however, the issue is not whether homosexuality is a disorder; the only issue is whether a particular *homosexual* was capable of sustaining a *heterosexual* relationship like marriage.

B. Degrees Of Homosexuality

Kinsey and his associates in 1948 suggested the following scale that would describe points on a heterosexual-homosexual continuum:

0 exclusively heterosexual
1 predominantly heterosexual, only incidentally homosexual
2 predominantly heterosexual but more than incidentally homosexual
3 equally heterosexual and homosexual
4 predominantly homosexual but more than incidentally heterosexual
5 predominantly homosexual, only incidentally heterosexual
6 exclusively homosexual

Those people who are 1 and 2 on the scale are sometimes referred to as *facultative homosexuals;* those who rate 3 and 4 are *bisexual;* and those who are 5 and 6 on the scale are *obligatory homosexuals.*

C. A Jurisprudence

1. *Severity*

In speaking of the severity of homosexuality several points must be clarified. First of all we are speaking always of genuine homosexuals and not pseudo homosexuals (heterosexuals who, in circumstances where opposite sex partners are not available, turn to persons of the same sex for gratification). Secondly whereas Alcohol Dependence is defined as including overt acts of drinking, homosexuality is defined apart from any overt acts, simply as "a strong preferential erotic attraction." This obviously involved the jurisprudential judgment that the erotic homosexual attraction, even without there being any overt acts, is likely to interfere substantially with functioning in an intimate heterosexual relationship, whereas totally controlled alcoholism is not. Thirdly, it can be said, as a rule of thumb, that obligatory homosexuals and bisexuals would probably be incapable of marriage, whereas facultative homosexuals would probably be capable. Here again, though, an attempt must be made in every individual case to determine the competence of the homosexual to function in a heterosexual relationship.

2. *Antecedence*

When a person is known to be homosexual, the homosexuality may always be presumed antecedent to marriage since a person's psychosexual preference is always fixed at least by early adolescence.

3. *Perpetuity*

Whenever homosexuality does, in fact, destroy a marriage, even if it be some years into the marriage, then the person may be regarded as having been incompetent for marriage at the time of the exchange of consent since he or she was, at that time, incapable of assuming the perpetual obligations.

4. *Relativity*

The choice of marriage partner by a homosexual can sometimes be significant. A female homosexual, for example, might function less well with an aggressive husband than with a gentle, passive man. It is always possible, therefore, that a homosexual condition not invalidating in itself could, given the wrong partner, result in an inability of the two parties to relate.

IGNORANCE

A. The Pertinent Canon

C. 1096 §1. For matrimonial consent to be valid it is necessary that the contracting parties at least not be ignorant that marriage is a permanent consortium between a man and a woman which is ordered toward the procreation of offspring by means of some sexual cooperation.

§2. Such ignorance is not presumed after puberty.

B. Ignorance And The Essence Of Marriage

The essence of marriage includes two elements, the *personalist* element, the joining of souls, and the *procreational* element, the joining of bodies.

The canon indicates that substantial ignorance regarding either element can invalidate a marriage.

C. Ignorance Regarding The Joining Of Souls

1. The canon notes that the parties must not be ignorant that marriage is a *permanent consortium between a man and a woman.*

2. This would seem to require that the parties recognize some personalist aspect to marriage, that the parties are not merely working together or producing together as fellow citizens, but are human, heterosexual partners.

3. If, therefore, a man were to view marriage simply as a contract by which he hired a housekeeper or social secretary and not as a true partnership involving fundamental equality, it would seem that the marriage could be declared null on the grounds of ignorance.

D. Ignorance Regarding The Joining Of Bodies

1. The canon notes that the parties must not be ignorant that marriage is *ordered toward the procreation of offspring by means of some sexual cooperation.*

2. Regarding the specific meaning of that phrase, the following observations might be made regarding insufficient and sufficient knowledge of the procreational aspects of marriage.

   a. *Insufficient* - there are two categories of ignorance about the joining of bodies which render a marriage invalid:

      1) *When it is judged that marriage entails no right to the body whatsoever.* And in this case other accidental knowledge can never render the marriage valid. A girl for example might under-

stand that she becomes pregant and gives birth. She might even understand that boys are different from girls, perhaps like roses are different from tulips. But if, in spite of all this, she judges that marriage does not mean that she must give to her husband the right to her body (if for example she thinks generation is spontaneous or God implants the seed or the stork brings the baby) the marriage is invalid.

2) *When it is judged that some right to the body is transferred but one that is substantially different from the real one.* If, for example, a girl thinks that she has given her husband only the right to give her a fertility pill or an injection or to breathe on her in some mysterious way or to employ some magnetic power or if she thinks that the marriage right consists in a warm embrace, then the marriage is null because although she has given him some right to her body it is substantially different from the substance of the matrimonial action.

b. *Sufficient* - On the other hand the marriage is valid if the person knows that *the physical coming together is placed by certain specific organs which are apt for and proper to generation, even though the identity of these organs is not clearly understood.* If the woman knows this much she is not erring about the substance of the action and at the same time the marriage right for her is sufficiently unique. She understands that she is giving to her husband a very special right, something more, for example, than the warm embrace she might give her brother.

3. The following practical criteria may be of some use in determining the presence of invalidating ignorance regarding the right to the joining of bodies.

a. *The Psycho-Physical Criterion* - ignorance is more likely present in the person who matures late and who has subnormal sexual drives than it is in the average person.

b. *The Educational Criterion* - ignorance is more likely present in people whose parents were extremely severe and strict disciplinarians and in people who tend to be asocial than it is in the average person.

c. *The Prenuptial Criterion* - ignorance is more likely present in people who were pushed into marriage or who were silly and immature during their courtship than it is in others.

d. *The Postnuptial Criterion* - shyness or even shame on the occasion of the first attempt at intercourse is not considered particularly indicative of anything. If, however, there was an easy adjustment to the initial surprise at discovering the nature of intercourse, then the presumption is that there was no ignorance about the giving of the matrimonial right, whereas, if there was a horror or repugnance or if the woman could not be persuaded to have intercourse even after being patiently and gently instructed by her husband, then the presumption is that she was truly ignorant, that she didn't think that she had given her husband that right, and the presumption therefore favors nullity.

E. Proof Of Ignorance

The usual proofs: declarations of the parties, affidavits, testimony of witnesses (see the pertinent canons in the simulation chapters) and circumstantial evidence (especially the person's family environment) should be utilized in a case of ignorance.

IMPOSED ERROR

A. The Pertinent Canon

C. 1098 — A person contracts invalidly who enters marriage deceived by fraud, perpetrated to obtain consent, concerning some quality of the other party which of its very nature can seriously disturb the partnership of conjugal life.

B. Some Observations On The Canon

1. This is a canon on error, not on fraud or deceit. This is clear from the fact that, according to the canon, it is not the *deceiver* (the one who perpetrates the fraud) but the *deceived* (the one who is in error) who contracts invalidly.

2. Nevertheless, fraud or deceit is an essential element here. Indeed, in Latin the ground is usually referred to as "error dolosus." In English we might refer to it as "imposed error."

3. Although the deceiver will usually be the other party, the canon does not require that that be so. Conceivably the deceiver or defrauder could be a third party.

C. Criteria

Specific criteria that must be met in order for error to be invalidating are the following:

1. The quality must be a *true* quality, i.e. an inherent feature or property of the person, as opposed to some isolated past action. If, for example, a party had had intercourse with another person prior to marriage, that would not be considered a true quality. Whereas if one had had a criminal record or had been a prostitute or had been in a previous civil marriage, these would be considered true qualities.

2. The quality must be *present* at the time of marriage, as opposed to a hoped for, future quality. If, for example, a woman married a man because he said he hoped to be a doctor or a millionaire, even though in fact he had no such hopes, this would not be invalidating. Whereas, if the man passed himself off as *really being* a doctor or millionaire at the time of the marriage when in fact he was far from it, then this could be invalidating.

3. The quality must be *unknown*. If, therefore, the deceived party either learns of the quality independently or strongly suspects the existence of the quality, then error cannot be said to be present, and the marriage cannot be considered invalid on this ground. Because, in effect, the deceived party is no longer deceived. A practical test for determining whether the quality was truly unknown at the time of the marriage would be whether the person reacts with surprise and bewilderment on discovery of the quality.

4. The quality must be one *which, by its very nature, has a potential for being seriously disruptive.* It bears noting that the canon does not require that the quality be, by its very nature, serious, but only that it have, by its very nature, a potential for being seriously disruptive. This could refer to any serious, i.e. grave quality, whether the gravity be objective or only subjective.

    A quality is considered to be *objectively* grave when society would regard its concealment or misrepresentation as a grave injustice to the other party. This would include such qualities as serious or contagious diseases, addictions to vice which would be seriously disruptive of marital harmony though perhaps not invalidating in themselves, a totally unacceptable reputation, etc. It would not include such qualities as being a heavy smoker or poor dancer, etc.

    A quality is *subjectively* grave when the deceived person has such an extraordinary, perhaps excessive, esteem for that attribute that although light in itself, it is nevertheless valued by the person as seriously desirable. It may happen, for example, that a woman is vigorously opposed to marrying a man addicted to heavy smoking. Perhaps because several of her friends and relatives have died from lung cancer. She tells her fiancé that she would never marry such a man and receives from him the assurance that in fact he doesn't smoke at all, only to discover later that he deceived her. In such a case the quality, although objectively light, *could* be considered grave.

5. The quality must be *fraudulently concealed in order to obtain consent.* Simple error about a quality, as C. 1097 §2 notes, is not ordinarily invalidating, but imposed error is. A couple may marry, for example, thinking they are in good health. Shortly after marriage, however, the man discovers that he has had multiple sclerosis for some time and will shortly be invalided. This quality is certainly extremely grave. It changes the whole marriage. The marriage, however, must be considered valid, since the couple presumably married unconditionally, in sickness and in health. If, however, the man knew all along that he had MS but fraudulently concealed it, the marriage would be null because the fraud constituted a grave injustice against the other person and deprived her of her freedom of choice.

D. Proof Of Imposed Error

In investigating imposed error a court looks to the usual sources: the declarations of the parties and testimony of witnesses (see canons in the chapters on simulation), circumstantial evidence (whether there is a history of deceit, whether special marriage arrangements were made to avoid detection), a motive (the basis for the deceiver's judgment that the other person would not marry were the quality revealed) and perhaps documents (a record of a previous civil marriage, a medical record showing prior awareness of a debilitating or genetic disease).

E. Retroactivity Of The Canon

Since C. 1098 has no counterpart in the 1917 Code, the question arises "Does the canon apply only to those marriages which were entered after November 27, 1983 (the effective date of the Code) or is the canon a declaration of natural law and so retroactive?" Because the canon is very broad and even envisions the possibility that the fraud might be perpetrated by a third party without the knowledge of either of the spouses, the answer is not a simple one. It seems rather that the judge must examine each case on its merits. In some instances the judge may legitimately conclude that invalidity is based on the natural law itself (and so applies to marriages that predate the 1983 Code) while in other cases it will appear that invalidity is based solely on this positive law of C. 1098 (and so would not apply to marriages contracted before November 27, 1983). See Appendix Four on p. 168.

F. Applicability Of The Canon

A question allied to retroactivity is applicability: Does C. 1098 apply only to the marriages of Catholics (i.e. marriages in which at least one party is Catholic — C. 1059) or does it apply to all marriages? Once again the answer is not a simple one. If the deceit and error are so gross that it may legitimately be concluded that invalidity is based on the natural law itself, then, of course, it would apply to all marriages. If, however, the deceit and error are more subtle so that invalidity would come only from ecclesiastical law, then it would, according to C. 11, affect only the marriages of Catholics.

G. The Relationship Between Imposed Error And Condition

These two institutes are very closely allied (33, 529-530). When, for example, a man marries an alcoholic woman he may allege either that he was deceived or that he had placed a condition against marrying such a woman.

Circumstances, however, may suggest one or the other to be the preferable approach. For example, when deceit is high (the woman has completely concealed her problem) and awareness is low (he has no idea she has a problem) then ERROR is the likely grounds. But where awareness is high (he has strong suspicions that she is alcoholic) and deceit is low (she has indicated to him that she drinks too much) then it would seem preferable to handle the case on the grounds of a CONDITION.

TOTAL SIMULATION

A. The Pertinent Canon

C. 1101 §1. The internal consent of the mind is presumed to be in agreement with the words or signs employed in celebrating matrimony.

§2. But if either or both parties through a positive act of the will should exclude marriage itself, some essential element or an essential property of marriage, it is invalidly contracted.

B. Distinction Between Total And Partial Simulation

1. Some rotal auditors, notably Felici (43, 370), Pinna (47, 678) and Rogers (61, 748) have held that there is no distinction between total and partial simulation, because, in effect, "whoever simulates, simulates totally."

2. Most jurists, however, do recognize a distinction between total and partial simulation (see the decision of 1/29/81 coram Stankiewicz in D2 pp. 140-143). *Partial* simulation, they say, occurs when one or more of the three "bona," goods or blessings (the bonum prolis, bonum fidei or bonum sacramenti) is excluded; *total* simulation occurs when marriage itself, i.e. the marital partnership is excluded.

   The distinction has merit on two counts. First in the **psychological** order; since the *total* simulator is often aware of the non-existence of the marriage he has feigned contracting externally, while the *partial* simulator may think he has contracted a marriage, but one limited or defined according to his restricting intention. Secondly, in the **juridical** order; since, during the investigative process, it allows the court to focus on the specific area in which the defective consent actually exists.

3. The 1983 Code, like the 1917 Code, does not speak of a distinction between total and partial simulation. It speaks rather of excluding a) marriage itself, b) an essential element or c) an essential property.

   a. *Marriage Itself.* Marriage is a "covenant by which a man and a woman establish between themselves a partnership of their entire lives, a partnership which is, by its nature, ordered to the good of the spouses and to the procreation and education of children" (C. 1055 §1).

   b. *Essential Elements.* The Relatio for the October 1981 meeting (p. 258) noted that the essential elements of marriage "are to be determined by doctrine and jurisprudence, taking into consideration the definition of marriage [in C. 1055 §1] and, indeed, the whole of legislation and doctrine, both juridic and theological." For present purposes, however, it may be said that the essential elements of marriage are two: the procreational element and the personalist element. The procreational element involves the right to intercourse. The personalist element involves the right to self revelation, understanding and loving.

    c.   *Essential Properties*. The essential properties of marriage are unity and indissolubility (C. 1056).

4.   An element is a part; a property is a characteristic. The elements of water are hydrogen and oxygen. The properties are liquid and clear. The constitutive parts (the *elements*) of marriage are the rights to the joining of bodies and souls, which rights are to be exchanged (the *properties*) exclusively and perpetually.

5.   Although the Code does not speak of a distinction between total and partial simulation, the distinction, because of its already noted psychological and juridical advantages, will no doubt continue to be utilized in jurisprudence and will be coordinated with the Code as follows:

Exclusion		Simulation	
Marriage Itself			} Total
Elements {	Personalist	Coniugum	
	Procreational	Prolis	
Properties {	Unity	Fidei	} Partial
	Indissolubility	Sacramenti	

C. Relationship Between Total And Partial Simulation

Generally speaking, the Rota has taken the position that if a marriage is null on the grounds of *total* simulation, it is also null on the grounds of *partial* simulation in respect to any and all of the three bona. Grazioli, for example, said, "the exclusion of children is automatically proved from the fact that total simulation is admitted" (33, 692). Furthermore, as we have seen, auditors like Felici, Pinna and Rogers would even argue in reverse, namely that if a marriage is null on the grounds of *partial* simulation, it is also null on the grounds of *total* simulation. In fact, however, the Rota did in one case give an affirmative decision on total simulation and a negative on partial simulation because a specific intention against children had not been proved. See 35, 637.

D. The Essence Of Total Simulation

1.   Total simulation is the act of *externally* feigning consent during a marriage

ceremony while *internally* excluding marriage or the right to the partnership of life.

2. True simulation always involves the finis operis (the inherent purpose of something) being excluded by and not just coexisting with the finis operantis (the purpose the individual has in mind, which is sometimes different from and extraneous to the finis operis).

To use a homely, non marital example: the finis operis of a gun is to shoot or fire. A gun is for shooting. It may, however, be legitimately used as a decorative piece, and when so used the finis operantis of the gun is to decorate a room. These two purposes, fines or ends may coexist. It may also happen, however, that the finis operantis completely thwarts, frustrates and blocks the finis operis. This would happen explicitly if the firing pin of the gun were removed. It would happen implicitly if the gun were under sealed glass or somehow made unreachable so that, in effect, the finis operis could not be used. In such cases where the finis operis of the gun is explicitly or implicitly excluded, the object is no longer a real gun but rather a simulated, fake or imitation gun.

The same can happen in marriage. The finis operis of marriage is a partnership of spouses that is procreative. A person might have as his own finis operantis in entering marriage the attainment of wealth or prestige. And these two purposes (the purpose of marriage and the purpose of the individual) could plausibly coexist. When, however, a person, in marrying, positively excludes the communal, unitive aspect of marriage, when he does not give to his spouse the right to a sharing, intimate relationship, then the finis operis of marriage is excluded and such an arrangement is only a simulated, fake or imitation marriage (30, 344).

E. The Positive Act Of The Will

1. C. 1101 §2 notes that the exclusion must be by a "positive act of the will."

2. A positive act of the will may be either explicit or implicit but is certainly something more than a negative act of the will, that is to say, a non act. Perhaps another homely example will serve to illustrate. Before us on the table are two objects, one round, the other square. There are three ways for us to wind up without the round object. The first is to reject or discard it (a positive, explicit exclusion of the round object). The second is to select instead the square object (a positive, implicit rejection of the round object). The third is to do nothing, to choose neither (a negative exclusion of the round object).

3. The Code says that a positive exclusion of marriage as a partnership is invalidating. It implies that a negative exclusion is not invalidating but it does not actually say that. Accordingly, some jurists have suggested that an "inadequate commitment" to marriage may likewise be invalidating (for a

disussion of this point, see the articles by Brown and by Humphreys which are listed in the Selective Bibliography). This suggestion, however, has not met with widespread acceptance.

F.   Implicit Simulation

The excluding of marriage that is involved in simulation need not be actual or explicit to be invalidating. It suffices if the exclusion is virtual and implicit ("De Actu Positivo Voluntatis Quo Bonum Essentiale Matrimonii Excluditur" by Dinus Staffa in *Monitor Ecclesiasticus,* 1949, I, pp. 164-173).

2.   There are three principal ways in which marriage or the right to the partnership of life may be excluded implicitly:

a.   *By permanently excluding the right to cohabitation*

Cohabitation and partnership of life are two different things. In one sense, perhaps the more obvious sense, partnership of life implies something more than cohabitation, since cohabitation is something merely physical whereas partnership of life is something personal. In another sense, however, partnership of life is something less than cohabitation, in that a true partnership of life can be attained without actually cohabitating. Absence can, given the right circumstances, make the heart grow fonder.

Nevertheless, in practice, when one positively and permanently excludes cohabitation, he implicitly excludes the right to the partnership of life, and marriage itself, and therefore totally simulates (29, 740 and 39, 8).

Though this point was not always so clear (see "Marriage and Cohabitation" in *The Jurist,* 1967, 85-89, and the second edition of *Annulments,* pp. 68-71) it no longer presents a problem in jurisprudence.

b.   *By going through a marriage ceremony solely for an extraneous reason*

Occasionally a person will go through a marriage ceremony only as a means to an end. He marries solely and exclusively for a reason that is extraneous to the finis operis of marriage. A man, for example, is in jail because of rape. He can gain release by marrying. He does go through the ceremony but only so that he can get out of prison (54, 50 coram Doheny). Or a man is in prison and in need of medical attention not available to prisoners. He marries only so that he can get out and obtain the desired medical treatment (58, 938 coram Filipiak). Or a woman marries solely to get away from home and escape the cruel domination of her father (52, 171 coram Lefebvre). Or a man marries a

92

pregnant woman solely to escape the wrath of her family or friends (55, 44 coram Lefebvre). Such marriages can be declared null when it is proved that the finis operis of marriage was effectively frustrated.

It may also happen in such cases that the simulator enters marriage with a certain amount of repugnance. The repugnance, however, is not what invalidates the marriage. Repugnance, in itself, is not invalidating (36, 423). It is the implicit simulation that invalidates.

c. *By substituting for true marriage one's own idea of marriage*

A person could simulate marriage by entering something different from marriage. In so doing he implicitly excludes the true essence or formal object of marriage. A man, for example, might view marriage purely as a contract by which he hires for himself an attractive social companion and hostess, and nothing more (see the decision of August 19, 1914 coram Sincero in AAS VII, pp. 51-56). Or a man might view the purpose of marriage as the attainment of a perfect spiritual unity between the spouses with children entering the picture only after that perfect spiritual unity has been achieved. If that in fact was what the man was consenting to at the time of the ceremony, even if he were to do it in good faith, the marriage could be declared null on the grounds of total simulation, since, in effect, the man was positively, if implicitly, excluding true marriage (57, 29 coram Pucci. See also 55, 764 for an interesting law section by Anné).

G. Proof Of Simulation

The principal factors that would be pertinent to proving total simulation are the following: 1) Declarations of the Parties, 2) Affidavits, 3) Testimony of Witnesses, 4) Circumstantial Evidence, and 5) Motive.

1. *Declarations of the Parties*

The value of the declarations of the petitioner and respondent in a marriage case is adequately summarized in the following canons:

C. 1535 - A judicial confession is a written or oral assertion against oneself made by any party regarding the matter under trial and made before a competent judge, whether spontaneously or upon interrogation by the judge.

C. 1536 §2 - In cases which concern the public good . . . a judicial confession and the declarations of the parties which are not confessions can have a probative force to be evaluated by the judge along with the other circumstances of the case; but complete probative force cannot be attributed to them unless other elements are present which thoroughly corroborate them.

C. 1537 - Having weighed all the circumstances, it is for the judge to evaluate the worth of an extra-judicial confession which has been introduced into the trial.

C. 1538 - A confession or any other declaration of a party lacks all probative force if it is proved that it was made through an error of fact or if it was extorted by force or grave fear.

2. *Affidavits*

Many courts obtain information from people by affidavit rather than by formal testimony. In general it may be said that affidavits are considered to have the same basic value as judicial declarations and testimony. But see also P, pp. 45 and 53.

3. *Testimony of Witnesses*

As regards the value of testimony by witnesses, the pertinent canons read:

C. 1572 - In evaluating testimony, after having obtained testimonial letters, if need be, the judge should consider:

1°   the condition and good reputation of the person;
2°   whether the witness testifies in virtue of personal knowledge, especially what has been seen and heard personally, or whether the testimony is the witness' opinion, or a rumor or hearsay from others;
3°   whether the witness is reliable and firmly consistent or rather inconsistent, uncertain or vacillating;
4°   whether the witness has supporting witnesses or whether there is support from other sources of proof.

C. 1573 - The deposition of a single witness cannot constitute full proof unless a witness acting in an official capacity makes a deposition regarding duties performed ex officio or unless circumstances of things and persons suggest otherwise.

For a brief but interesting law section on the use of one witness, see the decision of June 19, 1972 coram Pinto (64, 354-355).

4. *Circumstantial Evidence*

There is a whole range of circumstances which might lend plausibility or credence to the allegation of total simulation. The particular circumstances will depend on the case but some of the more common circumstances that might have relevance are: a certain amount of pressure being exerted on the alleged simulator, unhappy family relationships, a very brief marriage, the constant intent prior to marriage to marry someone else, a previously expressed intention never to marry, and a philosophy of life radically different from the Christian philosophy.

5. *Motive*

Just as every effect must have a cause, so every act of simulation must have a motive. To identify that motive goes a long way towards proving that the simulation did in fact take place.

It is always important, though, to distinguish the motive for simulating from the motive for going through the ceremony. A man, for example, might marry a woman for her money. That's the motive for *contracting*. If, however, he has, at the same time, a strong aversion for the woman, that becomes his motive for *simulating*. The principal aim always is to identify the motive for simulating. If, however, the motive for contracting is unworthy or unsuitable, this is not at all irrelevant, and should be considered as important circumstantial evidence. See also 64, 181-182.

Some of the more common motives for simulating are that the person already loves somebody else, he doesn't love his spouse or has an aversion to her, the spouses are of disparate social and educational classes, pre-marriage bickering, and occasionally just plain irresponsibility.

A. The Pertinent Canon

C. 1101 §1 - The internal consent of the mind is presumed to be in agreement with the words or signs employed in celebrating matrimony.

§2 - But if either or both parties, through a positive act of the will, should exclude . . . some essential element of marriage, it is invalidly contracted.

B. The Right To The Conjugal Act

1. The Code does not define what the essential elements of marriage are. It may, however, be deduced from C. 1055 §1, which states that the marital partnership is, "by its nature, ordered to the procreation and education of children," that one of the essential elements of marriage is the right to the conjugal act. See also C. 1061 §1.

2. The title of this chapter, "Intention Against Children" is a popular and somewhat inaccurate phrase. The right to *children* is not really exchanged in marriage. When a sterile man marries, for example, he cannot really give the right to chidren. This, however, does not invalidate the marriage. The right that *is* exchanged in marriage is the right to the conjugal act, and the sterile man is perfectly capable of that.

3. The right to the conjugal act binds at all reasonable times. It is obvious that the right to have intercourse in public is not exchanged in marriage. That would not be a reasonable time. If, therefore, that were excluded at the time of marriage it would not invalidate the marriage. However the meaning of the phrase "at all reasonable times" is not always so clear. Would a man, for example, have the right to noncontraceptive intercourse with his wife when he had been advised that another child might endanger her life, or when the couple could only with great difficulty support any more children? A court is occasionally called upon to answer such questions in its attempt to determine whether "the right to the conjugal act" had truly been excluded.

4. Besides the right to intercourse at all reasonable times, the term "the right to the conjugal act" also includes the obligation of not impeding procreation and life. If therefore a woman, for example, intended to perform the marital act in a natural way but also intended always to use spermicides or pessaries or to take the morning after pill or to practice abortion or infanticide, she would be marrying invalidly, because the obligation of not impeding procreation and life is implied in the "right to the conjugal act," a positive exclusion of which invalidates marriage (49, 81).

C. Excluding The Right To The Conjugal Act

Many couples entering marriage these days do so with an agreement to postpone children for a while. Such an agreement, however, does not usually involve an exclusion of "the right to the conjugal act." The following remarks are made, then, in an effort to clarify when the right is excluded and when it is not.

1. The essential terms of the marriage covenant are not determined by the parties. They are predetermined by God, nature and society. The marriage covenant therefore enjoys a certain constitutional integrity, even a sacred integrity or wholeness. Visually it may be represented by a perfect circle or pie, with one essential piece of the pie being the right to the conjugal act.

2. Generally when a couple enters marriage with an agreement to postpone children for a while, say for two years, their agreement leaves the covenant (the pie) untouched. The covenant remains whole and entire, and the right to the conjugal act (a piece of the pie) is therefore not excluded but exchanged. What the couple does is enter a kind of side agreement, extrinsic to the marriage covenant. At the same time, however, they realize the superiority and prevailing power of the marriage covenant so that in a showdown they would recognize that the rights exchanged in the marriage covenant prevail over their private, subordinate arrangement. If, therefore, one of the parties, say the wife, decided after six months or a year that she wanted children right away, it would be expected that her husband, recognizing that that was her marital right, would acquiesce. Perhaps he would do so reluctantly. Perhaps he would even remind her of their private agreement. But if he eventually acquiesced it would be a sign that he recognized the prevailing power of the marriage covenant (where the right to the conjugal act was granted) over the private agreement of the parties.

    It is, at any rate, always presumed that the marriage covenant remained intact, even where there is evidence that the couple had made a premarital agreement to postpone children. Like all presumptions, this one of course cedes to the truth, but in the absence of contrary evidence, the covenant is presumed to have been entered intact, and the marriage therefore entered validly.

3. Occasionally, however, the intent of one or both parties is so firm, intense, inflexible, and non negotiable, that it can no longer be viewed as a side agreement subordinate to the marriage covenant. In such a case the intention of that person invades the heart of the covenant itself, excludes from it the right to the conjugal act (extracts that piece from the pie), and thereby distorts, truncates and intrinsically limits the terms of the covenant. Should a man with such an intention, having entered marriage with the understanding that children would be postponed for say two years, be asked by his wife for a child after only six months, it could be expected that he would see his wife's request as an illegitimate extension of her rights and something for which he had not really bargained in entering marriage.

    This man would have truly excluded the right to the conjugal act and so entered marriage invalidly.

4.   Where the right to the conjugal act is truly excluded, even if it is done only for a period of time, the marriage is invalid. See the decision coram Davino of 12/13/78 in D2, pp. 149-152.

5.   Although the "positive act of the will" by which a person simulates can be implicit, this would seem to have little practical relevance when it comes to excluding the right to the conjugal act. Except for the case where cohabitation itself is excluded, when children are excluded they are excluded explicitly.

D. Proof That The Right To The Conjugal Act Has Been Excluded

The principal factors that would be pertinent to proving an intention against children are the following: 1) Declarations of the Parties, 2) Affidavits, 3) Testimony of Witnesses, 4) Circumstantial Evidence, 5) Motive, 6) Presumptions.

1.   *Declarations of the Parties*

The value of the declarations of the petitioner and respondent in a marriage case is adequately summarized in the following canons:

C. 1535 - A judicial confession is a written or oral assertion against oneself made by any party regarding the matter under trial and made before a competent judge, whether spontaneously or upon interrogation by the judge.

C. 1536 §2 - In cases which concern the public good . . . a judicial confession and the declarations of the parties which are not confessions can have a probative force to be evaluated by the judge along with the other circumstances of the case; but complete probative force cannot be attributed to them unless other elements are present which thoroughly corroborate them.

C. 1537 - Having weighed all the circumstances, it is for the judge to evaluate the worth of an extra-judicial confession which has been introduced into the trial.

C. 1538 - A confession or any other declaration of a party lacks all probative force if it is proved that it was made through an error of fact or it was extorted by force or grave fear.

2.   *Affidavits*

Many courts obtain information from people by affidavit rather than by formal testimony. In general it may be said that affidavits are considered to have the same basic value as judicial declarations and testimony. But see also P, pp. 45 and 53.

3. *Testimony of Witnesses*

As regards the value of testimony by witnesses, the pertinent canons read:

C. 1572 - In evaluating testimony, after having obtained testimonial letters, if need be, the judge should consider:

1°   the condition and good reputation of the person;
2°   whether the witness testifies in virtue of personal knowledge, especially what has been seen and heard personally, or whether the testimony is the witness' opinion, or a rumor or hearsay from others;
3°   whether the witness is reliable and firmly consistent or rather inconsistent, uncertain or vacillating;
4°   whether the witness has supporting witnesses or whether there is support from other sources of proof.

C. 1573 - The deposition of a single witness cannot constitute full proof unless a witness acting in an official capacity makes a deposition regarding duties performed ex officio or unless circumstances of things and persons suggest otherwise.

For a brief but interesting law section on the use of one witness, see the decision of June 19, 1972 coram Pinto (64, 354-355).

4. *Circumstantial Evidence*

The court should take into consideration all those circumstances which, though not probative in themselves, nevertheless cast light on the intentions of the people. Some circumstances that might be relevant would be the following: the fact that the couple was quarrelling before marriage giving rise to doubts about the happy outcome of the marriage, an excessive concern for material things, being uncomfortable with children and showing impatience with them.

5. *Motive*

Simulation cannot be considered demonstrated unless it is apparent from the acts that there was sufficient motive for simulating. Motives for excluding children would be an inordinate fear of childbirth on the part of the woman or the fear of losing her figure, the fear of transmitting diseases, an aversion to children, being in love with another, the unwillingness to be tied down, the financial hardships that would result, a conviction that one should not contribute to an already overpopulated world.

Oftentimes the crucial question to be answered by the court is whether the agreement to postpone children was just a subordinate agreement or whether it was so intense that it actually entered into the central contract and altered the sacred terms of the covenant. As an aid to answering that question it is often helpful to determine the subjective importance of the motive for simulating and compare it with the motive the person had for marrying (48, 409).

6. *Presumptions*

Here again, since the crucial issue is often the intensity of excluding children, the following three presumptions are valuable as indicators of intensity:

a. *Cause*

This presumption involves the decision to marry. What is envisioned is a discussion before final marriage plans are made. One party, the alleged simulator, say the man, asks the woman to agree to a postponement of children; she, hypothetically, does not agree. If the man would then have decided to go through with the marriage anyway, this suggests that his desire to postpone children was not really very intense, and the presumption therefore is that the right to the conjugal act was not excluded. If, on the other hand, it is clear that the man would have called off the marriage had the woman not agreed to a postponement, then the indication is that the intention was very firm indeed, and the presumption favors the conclusion that the right was excluded.

b. *Perpetuity*

We have seen that whenever the right to the conjugal act is truly excluded, even if it be only for a time, the marriage is invalid. Nevertheless, the intent to exclude children only for a time suggests a lack of intensity, so that the presumption favors the validity of the marriage. Whereas if the intent was to exclude children forever, then the presumption is that the very right to the conjugal act was excluded (28, 445; 39, 590; 66, 72-76).

Where the exclusion refers to an indefinite period of time, one must judge from all circumstances whether it should be considered temporary or permanent. For example, the phrase, "We will have children only after your father dies" could, depending on the circumstances, be either temporary or permanent. If the father were ninety years old it would be equivalent to a temporary exclusion but if the father were forty it would amount to a permanent exclusion. See the following Rotal citations: 32, 465 and 36, 328; 34, 715 and 37, 245; and also 24, 158; 34, 225; 40, 115; 47, 151 and 48, 409.

c. *Tenacity*

A tenacity or prolonged resistance to a partner wanting children gives rise to a presumption that the original intention entered into the heart of the contract and was primary and involved an exclusion of the right, whereas giving in to the wishes of the party without grave pressure suggests that the agreement about postponing children should be viewed as a side, subordinate agreement, and the presumption therefore favors the validity of the marriage (26, 36).

INTENTION AGAINST FIDELITY

A. The Pertinent Canon

C. 1101 §1 - The internal consent of the mind is presumed to be in agreement with the words or signs employed in celebrating matrimony.

§2 - But if either or both parties, through a positive act of the will, should exclude . . . an essential property of marriage, it is invalidly contracted.

B. The Right To Fidelity

1. C. 1056 notes that one of the essential properties of marriage is unity. Unity, however, at least in its strict sense, is a very basic right. It simply means that a person has the right to be the one and only spouse of the partner. The partner does not have the right to polygamy.

2. Fidelity is something different from unity. In the broad sense, marital fidelity refers to the trust, loyalty and support that spouses show each other. In the strict, juridic sense, it refers to sexual fidelity, i.e. having one's spouse as one's only sex partner. It means, therefore, that the partner lacks not only the right to have another spouse but the right to have another lover. The partner lacks the right not only to be a polygamist but to be an adulterer.

3. Historically, unity and fidelity have, in jurisprudence, always been seen as virtually identical. Over the past several decades, however, the link between the two qualities, though it has not been broken, has, as it were, been turned around. Or upside down. According to the older jurisprudence (33, 622; 39, 589; 51, 252) *fidelity was reduced* to mean unity; whereas, according to the newer jurisprudence (45, 641-642; 55, 717; 64, 101) *unity was extended* to mean fidelity.

4. Consequently, when C. 1134 speaks of marriage creating a "bond which is, by its nature, exclusive," it implies a twofold obligation: of unity *and* of fidelity.

5. The right to fidelity excludes the partner's right to engage in the sexual act with any other person, whether of the opposite or of the same sex. In theory, therefore, a marriage involving one homosexual partner could, conceivably, be heard on the grounds of an intention contra bonum fidei. In practice, however, the usual ground is lack of due competence.

6. Although the meaning of fidelity could, in theory, be extended to include the exclusive right to the joining of *souls,* it is difficult to imagine a case in which this would have any practical importance. In practice, therefore, fidelity always refers to the exclusive right to the joining of bodies.

When the right to the joining of souls, i.e. the right to the partnership of life, is excluded altogether from marriage, it is a matter of total simulation.

C. Excluding The Right To Fidelity

1. According to the *older* jurisprudence, the bonum fidei was excluded only when unity was excluded, i.e. only when the right to the conjugal act was given, cumulatively, to two people. According to the *newer* jurisprudence (which seems more in accord with the traditional understanding of the bonum fidei - see Friedberg, I, 1065, and *Casti Connubii*, 19-39), the bonum fidei is excluded when fidelity is excluded, i.e. whenever one intends not to bind oneself to sexual fidelity. See "The Jurisprudence of the Sacred Roman Rota: Its Development and Direction After the Second Vatican Council" by Aldo Arena, in *Studia Canonica*, 1978, 2, pp. 265-293.

2. In order to result in invalidity, fidelity must be excluded as part of the marriage covenant. It may happen, for example, that in entering marriage a man foresees and even intends that he will have an extramarital affair should he have the opportunity. If, however, this remains casual and incidental, his intention does not invade, and therefore does not vitiate, the covenant. If, on the other hand, his intention is so intense and important to him that it actually becomes part of his central agreement or exchange of rights, with the result that he would regard his wife's demands tht he be hers alone as an undue extension of the agreement he entered, then such a man excludes the very right to fidelity.

3. The positive act of the will by which fidelity is excluded can be hypothetical. If, therefore, a man intends as part of the marriage contract, to exchange the right to perpetual fidelity only if his wife remains sexually attractive to him, he contracts invalidly.

4. The positive act of the will can also be implicit. An implicit intention, however, must be distinguished from a presumed intention. An implicit intention is one that is expressed but not explicitly. A presumed intention is one which may or may not exist but is only conjectured to (56, 756-757). If, for example, a man had a lover both before and after marriage, one might presume that he did not intend to be faithful, but one could not say that those circumstances alone amounted to an implicit intention. On the other hand, if the man had a lover before marriage but was pressured into marrying someone else, openly expressed his aversion to marrying, spent more time, even in public, with his lover than with his wife, etc.; if, in other words, the circumstances became sufficiently forceful and clear that it could be said that his behavior truly expressed, though perhaps implicitly, the man's intention to withhold from his wife the right to fidelity, then the marriage could be declared null because of his implicit intention contra bonum fidei.

5. One's beliefs about free love and open marriage can be extremely influential in causing one to exclude, by a positive act of the will, the bonum fidei. C. 1099 notes that "error concerning the unity, indissolubility or sacramental dignity of matrimony does not vitiate matrimonial consent so long as it does not determine the will." Which implies that it *does* vitiate marriage if it *does* determine the will. In a contra bonum fidei case, then, the beliefs of the alleged simulator and the intensity of those beliefs, should always be carefully investigated by the court.

D. Proof That The Right To Fidelity Has Been Excluded

The principal factors that would be pertinent to proving an intention against fidelity are the following: 1) Declarations of the Parties, 2) Affidavits, 3) Testimony of Witnesses, 4) Circumstantial Evidence, and 5) Motive.

1. *Declarations of the Parties*

   The value of the declarations of the petitioner and respondent in a marriage case is adequately summarized in the following canons:

   C. 1535 - A judicial confession is a written or oral assertion against oneself made by any party regarding the matter under trial and made before a competent judge, whether spontaneously or upon interrogation by the judge.

   C. 1536 §2 - In cases which concern the public good . . . a judicial confession and the declarations of the parties which are not confessions can have a probative force to be evaluated by the judge along with the other circumstances of the case; but complete probative force cannot be attributed to them unless other elements are present which thoroughly corroborate them.

   C. 1537 - Having weighed all the circumstances, it is for the judge to evaluate the worth of an extra-judicial confession which has been introduced into the trial.

   C. 1538 - A confession or any other declaration of a party lacks all probative force if it is proved that it was made through an error of fact or it was extorted by force or grave fear.

2. *Affidavits*

   Many courts obtain information from people by affidavit rather than by formal testimony. In general it may be said that affidavits are considered to have the same basic value as judicial declarations and testimony. But see also P, pp. 45 and 53.

3. *Testimony of Witnesses*

As regards the value of testimony of witnesses, the pertinent canons read:

C. 1572 - In evaluating testimony, after having obtained testimonial letters, if need be, the judge should consider:

1°   the condition and good reputation of the person;
2°   whether the witness testifies in virtue of personal knowledge, especially what has been seen and heard personally, or whether the testimony is the witness' opinion, or a rumor or hearsay from others;
3°   whether the witness is reliable and firmly consistent or rather inconsistent, uncertain or vacillating;
4°   whether the witness has supporting witnesses or whether there is support from other sources of proof.

C. 1573 - The deposition of a single witness cannot constitute full proof unless a witness acting in an official capacity makes a deposition regarding duties performed ex officio or unless circumstances of things and persons suggest otherwise.

For a brief but interesting law section on the use of one witness, see the decision of June 19, 1972 coram Pinto (64, 354-355).

4. *Circumstantial Evidence*

Some of the circumstances that might be especially relevant in a contra bonum fidei case would be the moral and religious character of the person, whether the person was with his or her lover shortly before and shortly after marriage, whether he or she might have entered a marriage for an unworthy motive such as money, whether he or she might have been pressured into marrying, and whether promiscuity was present before and after marriage. On this latter point see the decision of 7/15/71 coram Pinto (63, 688-691). Should the promiscuity involve actual nymphomania or satyriasis (Don Juanism), then, of course, the likely ground would not be an intention contra bonum fidei but rather lack of due competence.

5. *Motive*

In order to regard an intention against fidelity as proved, the judge must be aware of the motive for simulating. Motives for excluding fidelity would be an attachment to a former lover, an inability to abandon a life of indulgence and promiscuity, and an aversion to one's spouse.

It is also helpful to compare the motive for simulating with the motive for entering a true marriage. Where the motive for simulating is very strong and the other weak, simulation may be presumed (48, 409).

INTENTION AGAINST PERPETUITY

A. The Pertinent Canon

C. 1101 §1 - The internal consent of the mind is presumed to be in agreement with the words or signs employed in celebrating matrimony.

§2 - But if either or both parties, through a positive act of the will, should exclude . . . an essential property of marriage, it is invalidly contracted.

B. The Meaning Of Perpetuity

1. The perpetuity of marriage refers to its indissolubility. It has been called the "bonum sacramenti" because of that special perpetuity enjoyed by the consummated *sacramental* marriage. Nevertheless, it is a property of all marriages, even non sacramental ones, since perpetuity belongs to the very essence of marriage (CC. 1056, 1057 §2 and 1134).

2. Perpetuity and permanence are two different things. Something is permanent when it is lasting or non-temporary. It is perpetual when it is everlasting or non-terminable (C. 1096 §1).

3. Permanence is a divisible notion. One could, for example, enter a permanent, that is, lasting contract, say for twenty five years, with an option to cancel after fifteen years. The option to cancel does not destroy the permanence of the contract since fifteen years would, in intself, be sufficiently stable and enduring to be regarded as permanent. Permanence, in other words, admits of degrees.

   Perpetuity, on the other hand, is an indivisible notion. It does not admit of degrees. A thing cannot be moderately perpetual or somewhat indissoluble. If it is even one degree less than perpetual it is not perpetual.

C. Excluding Perpetuity

1. Since perpetuity is an indivisible notion, one cannot hedge on indissolubility. One could intentionally hedge on children or fidelity and still keep his intention extrinsic to and subordinate to the integral marriage covenant (where the rights to children, fidelity and perpetuity are exchanged). A man, for example, can, in entering marriage, recognize that henceforth he is bound to be faithful to his wife, and he can, at the same time, intend perhaps to cheat if the opportunity presents itself. Or a couple may truly exchange the right to children and, at the same time, intend not to have the maximum number of children that the woman can physically bear.

   But if one intentionally hedges on perpetuity or indissolubility, the intention is automatically drawn into the covenant itself. If one decides that he will enter something less than an indissoluble, perpetual marriage, that decision or intention stands in direct and diametric contradiction to the terms of the marriage covenant. One cannot simultaneously intend on the one hand to enter an indissoluble marriage and on the other hand to enter a marriage that can be dissolved. One intention must necessarily cancel out the other. The two cannot exist side by side. A man cannot simultaneously give his wife a perpetual right to himself on the one hand and a terminable right on the other. The two are incompatible.

This means that, in excluding perpetuity, the intention need not have a special intensity, as it must in excluding children or fidelity. Because any genuine intention against perpetuity necessarily involves an intrinsic limitation or distortion of the marriage covenant.

2. Generally the exclusion of perpetuity is phrased hypothetically, as in "I plan to remain married for life if the marriage turns out to be a happy one." Even a hypothetical intention, however, suffices to invalidate a marriage (34, 809; 48, 256).

3. Perpetuity, furthermore, need not be excluded explicitly in order to result in nullity. An implicit exclusion suffices (56, 930-931). An implicit intention is not to be confused with a presumed intention (56, 756-757) but sometimes the circumstances are so unusual and compelling that the only reasonable conclusion that can be drawn from them is that indissolubility was excluded. Where, for example, a non Catholic man, already on record as believing in divorce, marries a woman he doesn't love in order to make another woman jealous, and then leaves his wife shortly after marriage, one may legitimately conclude that he excluded perpetuity from his marriage. Actions, after all, speak louder than words (facta sunt verbis validiora — 16, 50; 25, 61).

4. Finally a word about the effect that error about indissolubility might have on the validity of marriage. When a person begins by believing that divorce may and even should be utilized when a marriage is unhappy, what effect does that have on his intentions in entering marriage? To what degree does the intellectual error influence the will?

Over the past several years there has been a significant development of jurisprudence on this point. The older jurisprudence said that an erroneous belief about indissolubility almost always remains in the intellect and does not become a real act of the will (32, 110). The more recent jurisprudence, on the other hand, teaches that error does enter the will and presumptively results in an invalidating exclusion of perpetuity in two ways:

a. When the error amounts to a deep-seated, strong, conscious, firm, entrenched, stubborn conviction, and there is no reason to believe that the person would act in a way that would be inconsistent with or contrary to his conviction. This is the so called "error pervicax" or intransigent error.

b.   When the error, though real, is perhaps more moderate, less deeply rooted, but is, at the same time, joined to circumstances, such as a growing disenchantment prior to marriage, that would be likely to volitionalize the error.

For some significant rotal decisions regarding "determining error" see 46, 614; 49, 842; 53, 394; 56, 925; 60, 343, and 64, 682-684. See also the Filipiak and Pompedda decisions in D1, pp. 117-118 and D2, pp. 160-161. See also "The Exclusion of Indissolubility: Old Principles and New Jurisprudence" by David E. Fellhauer in *Studia Canonica*, 1975, 1, pp. 105-133.

The 1983 Code has phrased the matter (in C. 1099) this way, "Error concerning the unity, indissolubility or sacramental dignity of matrimony does not vitiate matrimonial consent so long as it does not determine the will." The canon seems to imply that error which *does* determine the will is, if not a ground of nullity in itself, at least an essential contributing element to the conventional ground of partial simulation contra bonum sacramenti. In practice, therefore, the total ground might be phrased as "error regarding and intention against perpetuity." See D2, p. 160.

In such cases it is not that the "positive act of the will" mentioned in C. 1101 §2 is missing; it is simply that the presence of the intransigent error amounts to a vehement presumption in favor of the conclusion that the person certainly acted in accord with his intransigent error and that he therefore excluded perpetuity by a positive (even if implicit) act of the will.

D.   Proof That Perpetuity Has Been Excluded

The principal factors that would be pertinent to proving an intention against perpetuity are the following: 1) Declarations of the Parties, 2) Affidavits, 3) Testimony of Witnesses, 4) Circumstantial Evidence, and 5) Motive.

1.   *Declarations of the Parties*

The value of the declarations of the petitioner and respondent in a marriage case is adequately summarized in the following canons:

C. 1535 - A judicial confession is a written or oral assertion against oneself made by a party regarding the matter under trial and made before a competent judge, whether spontaneously or upon interrogation by the judge.

C. 1536 §2 - In cases which concern the public good . . . a judicial confession and the declarations of the parties which are not confessions can have a probative force to be evaluated by the judge along with the other circumstances of the case; but complete probative force cannot be attributed to them unless other elements are present which thoroughly corroborate them.

C. 1537 - Having weighed all the circumstances, it is for the judge to evaluate the worth of an extra-judicial confession which has been introduced into the trial.

C. 1538 - A confession or any other declaration of a party lacks all probative force if it is proved that it was made through an error of fact or it was extorted by force or grave fear.

2. *Affidavits*

Many courts obtain information from people by affidavit rather than by formal testimony. In general it may be said that affidavits are considered to have the same basic value as judicial declarations and testimony. But see also P, pp. 45 and 53.

3. *Testimony of Witnesses*

As regards the value of testimony of witnesses, the pertinent canons read:

C. 1572 - In evaluating testimony, after having obtained testimonial letters, if need be, the judge should consider:

1° the condition and good reputation of the person;
2° whether the witness testifies in virtue of personal knowledge, especially what has been seen and heard personally, or whether the testimony is the witness' opinion, or a rumor or hearsay from others;
3° whether the witness is reliable and firmly consistent or rather inconsistent, uncertain or vacillating;
4° whether the witness has supporting witnesses or whether there is support from other sources of proof.

C. 1573 - The deposition of a single witness cannot constitute full proof unless a witness acting in an official capacity makes a deposition regarding duties performed ex officio or unless circumstances of things and persons suggest otherwise.

For a brief but interesting law section on the use of one witness, see the decision of June 19, 1972 coram Pinto (64, 354-355).

4. *Circumstantial Evidence*

Some of the circumstances that might be especially relevant in a case involving an alleged exclusion of indissolubility would be the religious background of the person, his age, the culture in which he was reared, the fact that he did not love the woman he married, a short lived marriage and subsequent remarriage and divorce, and, of course, the presence of an intensely held erroneous concept regarding indissolubility.

5. *Motive*

Among the motives that might make simulating plausible would be such things as being in love with a person other than one's spouse, a premarital realization that the couple is incompatible, a love of independence, and a deep seated conviction about the propriety of divorce as a solution to an unhappy marriage.

CONDITIONS

A. The Pertinent Canon

C. 1102 §1 - Marriage based on a condition concerning the future cannot be contracted validly.

§2. - Marriage based on a condition concerning the past or the present is valid or invalid, insofar as the subject matter of the condition exists or not.

§3 - The condition mentioned in §2 cannot be placed licitly without the written permission of the local ordinary.

B. Description Of A Condition

A condition, as the term is used here, is a circumstance attached to the marriage on which the validity of the marriage depends. In the *strict* sense it refers to a future circumstance which suspends the validity of a marriage. In the *broad* sense it refers to any circumstance, past, present or future, which immediately renders the marriage either valid or invalid.

The 1917 Code (C. 1092, 3°) recognized a future condition as a condition in the *strict* sense, i.e. as suspensive of validity. The 1983 Code (C. 1102, §1) sees a future condition as a condition in the *broad* sense, i.e. as immediately invalidating.

Therefore, prior to November 27, 1983 (the effective date of the 1983 Code) a future condition only invalidated the marriage if the condition was unfulfilled. After that date, a future condition invalidates a marriage immediately, even if the condition is later fulfilled.

C. Conditioning A Marriage

Popularly one thinks of a condition as something highly explicit, as phrased, for example, by "I marry you on the condition that you come into your inheritance within the first year of marriage." In fact a condition can be far more subtle than that. In investigating a possible condition a court should keep the following points in mind:

1. *A condition may be placed implicitly.*

Etymologically an implicit intention is one which is contained "in plico," i.e. in the folds of something else. In practice it refers to two different situations. The *first* is where the intention is expressed in words but only indirectly, as when a part is expressed in the whole, an effect in its cause, a species in its genus. When a man, for example, explicitly states that he will never cohabit with a woman, he implicitly simulates marriage. The *second* type of implicit intention is where the intention is expressed not in words but in actions, actions which can have no other meaning but that a certain intention was present motivating them. A man, for example, who says nothing but disappears immediately after the wedding ceremony never to be heard from again may be said to have excluded cohabitation implicitly (56, 929-931).

A condition, at any rate, need not be stated explicitly in order to invalidate marriage. An implicit condition suffices (49, 421).

2. *It is not required that a person placing a condition do so because of some doubt. Nor is a doubt required in order to prove a condition.*

Ordinarily, perhaps, it would not occur to a person to place a condition unless there were some suspicion about an important quality being missing. One would not usually say, for example, "I marry you only on the condition you are heterosexual" unless there was some doubt about the person's heterosexuality.

On the other hand, where a quality is extremely important to a person, he or she might want the validity of marriage to depend on that quality even without there being any real doubt about the existence of the quality. The Rota, for example, heard a case where the allegation was that the Catholic woman had married on the condition that the Calvinist man convert to Catholicism. Prior to the marriage the man promised her that he would become a Catholic, and she never doubted it. In fact the man never did convert. The Rotal judge, Monsignor Felici, judged that even without the doubt, the woman was such a good Catholic and having a Catholic husband was so important to her that the condition should be considered proved (48, 756).

3. *A person may place a condition without realizing that it results in the nullity of the marriage.*

On this point Monsignor Pinto said, in a decision of June 26, 1971 (63, 560):

> Jurisprudence, even Rotal jurisprudence, has sometimes held that a true condition can only be placed by a person who is aware of its invalidating effect. But this is not true. People are generally unaware of such legalities and in no way realize that entering marriage conditionally results in invalidity. All they know is that on occasion a particular circumstance is so important to them that they rate it higher than marriage itself and that, if they can't have the circumstance or quality, they don't want the marriage either. Now everybody agrees that that sort of mentality or intention conditions marital consent. And consequently Rotal jurisprudence, especially as it has evolved in recent years, holds that a true condition can coexist with ignorance of its invalidating effect as long as it is clear that the person would not have consented to marry unless the quality had been present.

4. *The value system both of society and of the individual is regarded as highly significant in determining the presence of a condition.*

In general jurisprudence has always recognized that, in order for a circumstance to be appropriate matter for a true condition, it ought to have a certain objective importance and it ought to be something that would play a significant part in the future life of the couple. Such circumstances would be, for example, the absence of venereal disease or of epilepsy or of sexual perversion.

Where, on the other hand, the circumstance is of only minor importance and would only indirectly affect conjugal life, such as a man's job or religion or social status, the presumption would be that a true condition is not present.

Our jurisprudence, though, has recognized too that sometimes the subjective estimate of a circumstance is not the same as the objective estimate. It may happen, for example, that a particular person regards his spouse's religion as extremely important. Wherever it is verified, therefore, that the circumstance is, in fact, of great importance to this particular contractant, then a true condition may well be present (40, 304; 49, 431; 50, 73).

5.   *In a future condition (for marriages prior to 11/27/83) it suffices if the circumstance will occur moderately soon and if it is moderately specific.*

As regards the fulfillment date of a condition, it should be pointed out that, on the one hand, a person cannot suspend the validity of the marriage indefinitely or forever (31, 416-417), and, on the other hand, the circumstance need not occur so soon as to eliminate, for all practical purposes, most contingencies that might be of concern to a person entering marriage (48, 741). It would be reasonable to expect that a "few years" time might be the outside limit for the fulfillment or non fulfillment of a condition.

As regards the degree of specificity required, a circumstance on the one hand need not be ridiculously specific (I marry you if you inherit $10,956.23), and on the other hand should be something more than a vague generalization (I marry you if something really good happens). But the circumstance should have a moderate, measurable, verifiable, realistic specificity (I marry you if you receive a substantial inheritance within the next few years).

It is clear from all this that the conditioning of a marriage can be very subtle indeed. It can be done implicitly, i.e. stated indirectly or only conveyed by actions. A condition may be placed simply because a person regards a particular circumstance as extremely important. It does not have to occur to the contractant that the validity of the marriage is at stake, and the circumstance itself can be something that is only fairly precise and which may be verified within a few years time.

Even though a condition may be subtle, however, it must, in order to be a true condition, fulfill the basic requirements of a genuine condition.

D. The Core Of A Condition

Put in its simplest terms a marriage is conditioned when people know that "a particular circumstance is so important to them that they rate it higher than marriage itself, and, if they can't have the circumstance or quality, they don't want the marriage either" (Pinto decision of 6/26/71 quoted above). When, in other words, the marriage is subordinated to the quality in a "nexus subordinationis" (51, 117 coram Lefebvre) or when the circumstance prevails over the marital consent (42, 150 and 51, 631 coram Mattioli; 43, 569 coram Felici), then a true conditioning of the marriage exists.

E. Allied But Distinct Situations

There are four situations which in some ways resemble a condition but which do not invade the covenant and which leave marriage absolute. They are:

1. *Mode* — an obligation attached to the covenant by which one party makes some postnuptial demand on the other, e.g. "I marry you but afterwards you must stop drinking."

2. *Demonstration* — the expression of some quality which is taken for granted in one's spouse, e.g. "I marry you who are a virgin."

3. *Cause* — the reason or motive for the marriage, e.g. "I marry you because you will become a Catholic."

4. *Postulate* — otherwise called a prerequisite or presupposition.

    a. The postulate has often been confused with the *cause* but is, in fact, quite different. A cause remains in the intellect as the reason for the marriage whereas a postulate is in the will and is a true condition which refers primarily to the initial decision to marry. As, for example, when a man says "I take you as my fiancée on the condition that you are a practicing Catholic."

    b. The postulate has also been likened to a *prematrimonial condition* which does not influence the marriage itself. Some people have said, in other words, that the postulate is more a condition attached to the engagement than a condition attached to the marriage. Once the man, for example, is convinced that his intended is a practicing Catholic and takes her as his fiancée, then that is the end of the effectiveness of the prenuptial condition. It may not be presumed, they say, that the man further desires the validity of the marriage to depend on that past condition. For that, a new will act would have to be made. Perhaps it could be said that the engagement was invalid but it certainly would not follow that therefore the marriage was also invalid. Presumably the marriage was entered absolutely.

    This, too, however, does not adequately express the true influence of the postulate.

c. In point of fact the postulate is more correctly regarded as the *initial step* towards a matrimonial condition. In the real world, in other words, if a man becomes engaged to a woman only on the condition that she is a practicing Catholic, then more than likely, particularly if the prematrimonial condition was placed with considerable intensity, the postulate does influence, perhaps indirectly and secondarily, but nevertheless does influence the marriage itself (49, 420).

F. A Personalist Condition

Everyone realizes that a great many people today enter marriage primarily for personal fulfillment. Personal fulfillment, it would seem, would enjoy a sufficient degree of specificity to qualify as a circumstance that might condition a marriage. It is, at least in many instances, measurable and verifiable. If, for example, it turns out, after a year or so of marriage, that a couple is hardly communicating at all except to argue, it can be reasonably concluded that personal fulfillment is lacking.

If, therefore, it can be shown in a specific instance, that a party attached prevailing importance to personal fulfillment and subordinated marriage to it, that if personal fulfillment wasn't being realized within a few years after marriage the person didn't want the marriage either, such a marriage: 1) if it took place *before* 11/27/83 and the condition was unfulfilled, can be declared null by reason of C. 1092, 3°, 2) if it took place *after* 11/27/83, even if the condition was fulfilled, can be declared null by reason of C. 1102 §1.

G. Proof Of A Condition

In proving a condition the important factors to be considered are: 1) Declarations of the Parties, 2) Affidavits and Testimony of Witnesses, 3) Circumstantial Evidence, 4) Motive.

1. *Declarations of the Parties*

    The canons regarding the declarations of the parties as quoted in the four chapters on simulation are pertinent here. Also, although the exact words used by the contractant are important, nevertheless, since the word "condition" is so ambiguous (35, 793), and since, in general, actions speak louder than words (facta sunt verbis validiora — 16, 50; 26, 61) it is even more important to understand the total context and especially the mentality or mind set of the contractant (48, 742-743).

2. *Affidavits and Testimony of Witnesses*

    Here again the relevant canons can be found in any of the simulation chapters. It should be noted particularly, however, that if the witnesses relate the words of the contractant more forcefully than the conditioner himself, then the testimony of the witnesses must be regarded as exaggerated, according to the axiom that there cannot be more water in the rivers than there is at the source (non potest plus esse in rivis quam in fonte — 18, 233).

3. *Circumstantial Evidence*

Circumstances that might be important in proving a condition are whether the quality is objectively or only subjectively and perhaps idiosyncratically grave, the seriousness or solemnity used in expressing the condition, whether it was expressed only once or repeatedly, whether there was an attempt to impose it on the other party (34, 819). The quickness of terminating the marriage and seeking an annulment once it is realized that the condition has not been fulfilled might also be important, but it should be realized too that some conditions are fulfilled only gradually and equivocally and sometimes involve injuring the reputation of the other party, and in such a case a delay is more than understandable (50, 74).

4. *Motive*

The motive for conditioning a marriage is usually found in the extreme importance attached to the circumstance by the conditioner.

H. Relationship Between Condition And Conditioning Error (C. 1097 §2)

C. 1097 §2 says that when an error concerning a quality of a person is "directly and principally intended" the marriage is invalid.

This is in no way different from a condition. The core of a condition, as noted above under D, consists in the marriage itself being subordinated to a quality in a "nexus subordinationis." A woman, for example, marries a man, erroneously thinking that he is a Catholic. If her *principal* intention is to marry a Catholic (and her "less principal" or *subordinate* intention is marriage) then the marriage is null. The proper ground of nullity, however, is not error but condition (see Cappello, *De Matrimonio* n. 585, 2, 4° and the decision coram Stankiewicz of February 15, 1980, 72, 94).

I. Relationship Between Condition And Imposed Error (C. 1098)

These two institutes are very closely allied (33, 529-530). When, for example, a man marries an alcoholic woman he may allege either that he was deceived or that he had placed a condition against marrying such a woman.

Circumstances, however, may suggest one or the other to be the preferable approach. For example, when deceit is high (the woman has completely concealed her problem) and awareness is low (he has no idea she has a problem) then ERROR is the likely grounds. But where awareness is high (he has strong suspicions that she is alcoholic) and deceit is low (she has indicated to him that she drinks too much) then it would seem preferable to handle the case on the grounds of a CONDITION.

A. The Pertinent Canon

C. 1103 - A marriage is invalid if it is entered into due to force or grave fear inflicted from outside the person, even when inflicted unintentionally, which is of such a type that the person is compelled to choose matrimony in order to be freed from it.

B. Force

1. Force (vis) is the coercion (coactio moralis) which moves the will under the threat of an evil in such a way that the will, otherwise not about to consent, does, in order to avoid the evil, consent to the imposed action.

2. When this definition is applied to marriage, it is clear that the true consent which is the efficient cause of marriage is presumed to be present (coacta voluntas manet semper voluntas) so that the question may well be asked, "Why, if the efficient cause of marriage is truly present, is the marriage invalid?" The answer basically is that, in a forced marriage, the full freedom of a person to choose one's own spouse, which is a basic human right, is not respected (Gaudium et spes, nn. 17, 26, 27, 29, 48 and 52).

C. Common Fear

Fear (metus) is the intimidation (trepidatio mentis) which results from the force. In order to invalidate marriage, the fear must be grave, extrinsic, and causative.

1. Grave

    In order to invalidate marriage fear must be grave. It may, however, be either absolutely or relatively grave. Fear is *absolutely* grave when it arises from an evil which is capable of compelling a well-balanced person to enter marriage against his will. Evils of this sort are threats of death, mutilation, imprisonment, exile, loss of great wealth and disinheritance. Lesser evils inflicted on more timid people can result in fear which is *relatively* grave but always there must be some objective gravity, at least prudently feared, for otherwise (if the gravity is a pure figment of one's imagination) the fear is not really extrinsic but intrinsic (27, 211; 35, 196; 35, 319).

2. Extrinsic

    a. In its most obvious meaning this simply indicates that the fear is not invalidating if it is *intrinsic,* as for example, if it results from mere autosuggestion or suspicion or moral or social obligation or from a scrupulous conscience.

b.	It also means, however, that fear is not invalidating if it is caused by some *necessary or extra-human* agent, as for example, sickness, precarious economic situation or public infamy.

It should perhaps be noted here that when there is the intervention of an intermediary one must carefully ascertain whether he or she is advising the person of mere facts or of threats. If, for example, a doctor acts as a kind of intermediary in advising a woman that she is pregnant, the intervention of the doctor obviously does not make the fear extrinsic because it is not the doctor but the pregnancy which the woman fears. But if, on the other hand, it is the woman's brother, for example, who is advising her of the father's threats, then extrinsic fear is indeed present. See the following Rotal decisions: 17, 240; 18, 176; 26, 81; 31, 26; 35, 74.

3.	*Causative*

a.	In order to invalidate a marriage the fear must not only be grave and extrinsic; it must also be causative. That is to say, one must have been compelled to marry in order to free himself of the force and fear. Marriage, in other words, must be the effect, of which the cause (the principal and determining cause) was fear, so that if the fear (the cause) were not present, marriage (the effect) would not take place. It is clear then that to invalidate a marriage, fear ought not to be merely the occasion of marriage (so that one marries *cum metu*) but the real cause (so that one marries *ob* metum vel *ex* metu).

b.	If there is another remedy besides the marriage to the threatened evil, which remedy is not utilized, then it is presumed that there was another cause for the marriage, that fear was not the cause and that the marriage was not entered ex metu.

c.	The force need not be inflicted *directly* for the purpose of extorting consent. It is sufficient if the force is present and *indirectly* causes the marriage, e.g., when the father of a pregnant woman threatens, in anger, to kill the woman's lover, whereupon the lover offers to marry the woman. This was stated *implicitly* in the 1917 Code (in that it rejected a draft canon requiring direct force - see Coronata III, para. 479) and is stated *explicity* in the 1983 Code (by the phrase "even when inflicted unintentionally - etiam haud consulto incussum" - see Relatio, p. 258 and D2, p. 179).

d.	It should be noted, furthermore, that the words of the Code, "the person is compelled to choose matrimony," do not indicate a compulsion to a particular marriage with a specific person but to marriage in general. If, therefore, a person is truly compelled to marry to avoid some evil, the marriage is invalid even if some choice of spouses is offered.

e. In an interesting case decided before Mattioli on January 23, 1957, the Rota declared a marriage null in which the force exerted on the woman to go through a civil ceremony was regarded as virtually perduring and influencing the religious marriage four years later (49, 37).

f. Perhaps the best criterion for judging whether a marriage was entered ex metu or simply cum metu is the presence of aversion. This *could* mean a physical aversion for the person but need not; it suffices that there be an aversion to *marrying* this person. This type of aversion obviously could exist simultaneously with liking the person as a friend since there is a vast difference between wanting the person as a friend and wanting him as a husband. But unless there is some sign of this minimal type of aversion, the marriage must be considered valid.

The ordinary signs or symptoms of aversion are crying and complaining before marriage, sadness and denial of the signs of affection. The absence of such signs after marriage proves nothing since it is then presumed that one is making the best of a bad situation.

Where there *are* these signs, where there is aversion, fear is presumed, *only* presumed however and not with a certainty which would invalidate marriage. Ultimately it is not merely aversion but fear that must be proved.

D. Reverential Fear

1. *The Notion*

When the extrinsic force exerting the influence is a parent or some superior, the whole question of reverential fear and its special considerations comes into play. It is not that the net result of reverential fear is something different from the fear mentioned in C. 1103. It is simply that where we start off with a relationship of subjection, we have a kind of breeding ground, we have the ideal conditions for the existence of fear.

2. *The Object*

Obviously where the subject has a built-in respect, reverence and obedience for the superior, he or she is especially fearful of offending the superior and most of all of arousing the superior's indignation. It is important to note that it is this indignation and not any concomitant threats of evil which is the specific object of reverential fear. Thus, if a daughter is threatened by her father with expatriation, we have two evils which are exerting force—the indignation of the father and expatriation. If the daughter marries to avoid indignation she is marrying out of *reverential* fear. But if she marries to avoid expatriation, she is marrying out of *common* fear. It is not always easy, of course, to determine whether the expatriation is the *principal* motive for marrying, a *subsidiary* motive or just a *sign* of the father's indignation but it is an important area to be investigated by the court.

3. *The Degree*

This indignation which is the specific object of reverential fear would, in itself, be considered force or coercion but would per se be considered only slight coercion. If, however, it were or probably would be harsh or long lasting, it could easily be serious or grave coercion and could result in grave, invalidating fear.

4. *Parental Behavior*

This indignation is an abuse of authority and of the filial reverence offered by the children and is a luxury in which no parent has a right to engage. This is not to say, of course, that parents have no right to assist their children in choosing a partner, that they cannot offer them advice and even warnings, that they cannot attempt to persuade their children to marry this or that partner, even to the extent of using some moderate, proportionate force as long as it remained parental. All of this, indeed, may prompt the subject to sacrifice his or her own happiness and, in order to comply with the wishes of the parent, agree to marry, perhaps "non libenter sed libere tamen."

But this is quite different from inflicting a fear of harsh and long lasting indignation on one's child. Here the means are not the moderate urgings and exhortations mentioned above but severities, cruelties, absolute and imperious commands, threats, curses, a grim and gloomy mien, angry badgering, ceaseless and uncivil complaining, constant and annoying requests. These remove from the child the possibility of marrying "non tantum libenter sed etiam libere" (not necessarily eliminating free consent altogether but greatly diminishing the actual freedom and making the choice at best a voluntarium secundum quid, something which would not have been willed at all were it not for the fear).

5. *Another Remedy*

As regards the element of causality (C 3b), it should be noted that, in the case of reverential fear, the real evil present is the parental indignation, not the actual content of concomitant threats. In the case then of the girl who marries to avoid not the *expatriation* but the *indignation* of the parent, the question to be asked is not whether there was another remedy to expatriation but whether there was another remedy to indignation; not whether, if she hadn't married, she could have avoided the *expatriation* but whether, if she hadn't married, she could have avoided by any other remedy the *indignation* of her father.

6. *Extreme Force*

It should likewise be noted that if the force exerted on the subject is so grave that it would give rise to intimidation even in the non subject, then the resulting fear is not really reverential fear at all but common fear. It is clear therefore, that not all fear exerted by parents is reverential fear. Reverential fear and common fear differ in two ways: by reason of the *object* (indignation vs. something else) and by reason of *degree* (the amount likely to be exerted on a loved one vs. the kind used on a well balanced person who owes no reverence).

E. Proof Of Force And Fear

There are two basic arguments in a force and fear case: the direct argument (proving coercion) and the indirect argument (proving aversion).

In developing both arguments the Court should of course look to the declarations of the parties and the testimony of witnesses (the relevant canons can be found in the chapters on simulation), to all the circumstantial evidence (the age, sex and temperament of the one being forced, relationship to the person exerting the coercion, etc.) and to a motive for the coercion.

F. Applicability Of The Canon

The Code Commission, having determined apparently that the nullity caused by force and fear is of the natural law (for Rotal decisions on this matter see 40, 327-328; 56, 650 and 61, 284), has declared that C. 1103 can apply to non-Catholics as well as Catholics (*Communicationes*, 1987, 1, p. 149). For a more nuanced commentary on the Code Commission's response, however, see Urbano Navarrete's remarks in *Periodica*, 77, 1988, pp. 497-510.

DEFECTIVE CONVALIDATION

A. The Pertinent Canons

C. 1156 §1 - To convalidate a marriage which is invalid due to a diriment impediment, it is required that the impediment cease or that it be dispensed and that at least the party who is aware of the impediment renew consent.

§2 - This renewal of consent is required by ecclesiastical law for the validity of the convalidation even if both parties furnished consent at the beginning and have not revoked it later.

C. 1157 - The renewal of consent must be a new act of the will concerning a marriage which the person who is renewing consent knows or thinks was null from the beginning.

C. 1158 §1 - If the impediment is a public one, the consent is to be renewed by both parties according to the canonical form, with due regard for the prescription of canon 1127 §2.

§2 - If the impediment cannot be proven to exist, it is sufficient that the consent be renewed privately and in secret by the party who is aware of the impediment, provided the other party perseveres in the consent already given, or by both parties when each of them knows about the impediment.

C. 1159 §1 - A marriage which is invalid due to a defect of consent is convalidated when the party who had not consented now gives consent, provided the consent given by the other party still exists.

§2 - If the defect of consent cannot be proven it is sufficient that the party who did not consent gives consent privately and in secret.

§3 - If the defect of consent can be proven it is necessary that the consent be given according to the canonical form.

C. 1160 - With due regard for the prescription of canon 1127 §2, marriage which is invalid due to a defect of form must be contracted anew according to canonical form in order to become valid.

B. Those Bound By Ecclesiastical Law

The rules for determining who is and who is not bound by ecclesiastical law are, as we shall see, of some import in this area. In terms of a possible convalidation they may be summarized as follows:

1. *Under the 1917 Code*

    a. A Catholic was bound (C. 12)
    b. A baptized non-Catholic was bound (C. 12)
    c. A non-baptized person was bound only when marrying a baptized person (C. 1016)

2. *Under the 1983 Code*

    a. A Catholic is bound (C. 11)
    b. A baptized non-Catholic is bound only when marrying a Catholic (C. 1059)
    c. A nonbaptized person is likewise bound only when marrying a Catholic (C. 1059).

C. The Division Of The Canons

The canons on convalidation are divided into three sections, treating, namely, marriages which are null due to a:

1. Diriment Impediment (1156-1158)

2. Defect of Consent (1159)

3. Defect/Lack of Form (1160)

D. Convalidating Marriages Null Because Of A Diriment Impediment

The canons of both the 1917 and the 1983 Codes indicate that when a marriage is null because of a diriment impediment, it is validated by a) the cessation of the impediment, b) the person being aware that the marriage was null because of the impediment and c) the renewal of marital consent, i.e. a new decision to marry (expressed, when required, according to the norms of law) which involves the exchange of the essential marital rights in view of the fact that those rights had never before been exchanged, at least effectively.

The canons further indicate that the latter two factors (knowledge of nullity and renewal of consent) are required only by ecclesiastical law and are not therefore relevant when the marriage involves people not bound by that law.

There are then the following practical possibilities:

a. *Marriage Involving Two Unbaptized Parties* - Two Jewish people, for example, marry after one of them obtains a divorce from a previous spouse. The impediment of ligamen is present invalidating the union. Should the previous spouse die, however, the present marriage is ipso facto validated by the cessation of the impediment. Consequently, should the second marriage later break up and one of the parties wish to marry a Catholic, that second marriage could not be declared null on the grounds of a defective convalidation (or even of prior bond).

This has been the operative jurisprudence under both Codes.

b. *Marriage Involving Two Non-Catholics, at least One of Whom is Baptized*

1) *Under the 1917 Code* - Were one or both of the people in the case outlined above not Jewish but Protestant, then by reason of their baptism, they would, in order to validate their union on the death of the former spouse, first have had to recognize its invalidity and secondly have had to renew their consent (though not according to any particular form). Both of these requirements, though, would have been so unlikely to be met by a non-Catholic that once the initial marriage was proved invalid, its invalidity may be presumed to have perdured despite the cessation of the impediment.

2) *Under the 1983 Code* - After the 1983 Code went into effect this type of marriage followed the same rules as those that had previously applied to a marriage involving two unbaptized people (as in a. above). For example: two Protestants, Jack and Jane married in 1982 and were divorced in 1983. In 1984 Jane married Tarzan, another Protestant. That marriage was null by reason of ligamen. When, however, Jack died in 1985 the marriage of Jane and Tarzan was automatically validated.

c. *Marriages Involving at least One Catholic Party* - When a Catholic is involved it is less likely that a marriage will take place with a diriment impediment being present. It is conceivable, though, that a couple might marry with one of them, for example, being unbaptized or under age without a dispensation having been granted. In that event, if the impediment is *demonstrable* (public) then the marriage may be declared null informally unless and until consent is renewed in the proper form; and if the impediment is *not demonstrable* then the marriage cannot be declared null at all.

E. Convalidating Marriages Null Because Of Defect Of Consent (Or Force And Fear)

It is consent that makes marriage. When consent is lacking, there is no marriage. There is no substitute for consent. (C. 1057 §1). This is a matter not just of ecclesiastical law but of the natural law itself.

Therefore, when a marriage is null because of a defect of consent, i.e. because of some defect mentioned in the Code under the heading "De Consensu Matrimoniali" (embracing CC. 1095-1107), then the natural law would require that a genuine marital consent be elicited, which, as C. 1157 points out, would entail the person recognizing the invalidity of the first ceremony.

Consequently, whatever the baptismal or ecclesial status of the parties, were a marriage invalid because of, let us say, force and fear, it would not be ipso facto validated when the force and fear ceased but knowledge of nullity and renewal of consent would be required in order to validate it.

It was indeed on this very basis that the famous Vanderbilt-Marlborough marriage was declared null by the Rota. See 18, 286 and, for a similar case, 28, 714.

F. Convalidating Marriages Null Because Of Lack Of Form

C. 1160 is clearly speaking about marriages that involved at least one Catholic in which the form was neither observed nor dispensed. In convalidating such marriages, as noted in Section B, even the non-Catholic party has, under both the old and the new Code, been obliged to observe ecclesiastical law. In such cases, therefore, it is required that both parties a) personally recognize the nullity or at least the probable nullity of the former marriage and b) transfer the marital right to their partner, i.e. not merely confirm or reiterate a former exchange of rights but actually give a new marital consent distinct from the former inefficacious one.

This does not usually involve a problem where both parties are Catholic but these requirements demand more than can reasonably be expected of most non-Catholics. Consequently many convalidations involving a non-Catholic can be proved invalid on the grounds that the non-Catholic party either failed to recognize the original union as invalid or failed to give new consent.

Finally, it must be remembered that in these cases it is not necessary to prove simulation, i.e. exclusion of marital consent by a *positive* act of the will; but it is only necessary to prove the *negative* omission of the new consent required for a valid convalidation. See the decision of January 21, 1969 coram Rogers (61, 64-65) in D1, p. 144.

G. Proof Of Defective Convalidation

The declarations of the parties and the affidavits and testimony of witnesses (see the canons in the simulation chapters) are important in proving a defective convalidation. All records should likewise be obtained so that it is clear that a genuine convalidation is being considered. Also the circumstances that might be relevant, such as the religion of the parties, what, if any prenuptial preparation was given, the person's attitude toward the Catholic Church, the reason for the convalidation, how soon after the first marriage it occurred, and whether the parties were getting along well at the time.

APPENDICES

APPENDIX ONE

Canon 1095: A Bird's-Eye View

I. INTRODUCTORY REMARKS

Canon 1095 is a new creature; the 1917 code contained nothing like it. Basically it says that people who are not psychologically equipped for marriage cannot enter a valid marriage.

Canon lawyers, especially judges, are happy to have the canon. It is one of the important innovations in the new code. At the same time, however, it is quite clear that the canon, in and of itself, says almost nothing. It is very much like saying that one must be strong enough for the task. Well, of course! But the question is: what is the task?

In much the same way, canon 1095 tells us that a person must be strong enough for marriage. But the question is: what is marriage? It is a question that has been asked for centuries. The answer has not always been the same.

II. MARRIAGE BEFORE VATICAN II

There are two basic elements to marriage: the *procreational* element called the *"bonum prolis,"* and the *personalist* element, called the *"bonum coniugum."*

As the subject of marriage has been investigated over the centuries by various civil lawyers, canon lawyers and theologians, some have tended to emphasize the *procreational* element while others have emphasized the *personalist* element. Let us look briefly at a few examples of each.

A.   *Those Favoring the* Bonum Prolis

   1.   *St. Augustine* (d. 430). St. Augustine, as Theodore Mackin has pointed out,[1] was "caught in a kind of crossfire." He lived at a time when two extremist positions were tearing society apart. One opinion said, in effect, that all sex was bad, the other that all sex was good. Augustine attempted to find orthodoxy somewhere in between. Sex, he said, was sometimes good and sometimes bad. Usually bad perhaps. But sometimes good, namely when it is had within marriage for the purpose of procreating offspring.[2] Procreation, for Augustine, was the main point of marriage. Etymologically, he noted, the word matrimony is derived from the Latin word for mother —*mater.*[3] *Mater*-matrimony. When a couple marries, in other words, the woman becomes not so much a wife as a mother. Procreation is what counts. Indeed, in his final essay on marriage, Augustine spelled it out quite clearly. He said: "Therefore the propagation of children is the first, the natural and the legitimate purpose of marriage."[4]

This Augustinian attitude and theory on marriage was, as we know, immensely influential for hundreds and hundreds of years.

2. *Gratian* (1140). When Gratian composed his *Decretum,* he phrased the question in more legal terms than had Augustine but his conclusion was basically the same. In Cause 27 (the opening cause on the subject of marriage) he wrote, "Let us ask ourselves the question: which sort of consent constitutes marriage? Is it consent to cohabitation or to intercourse or to both?"[5]

Gratian's answer was that the consent that constitutes marriage is the consent to intercourse. Even the Virgin Mary, he said, consented to carnal intercourse. If she had not, he implied, she would not have been truly married.[6] Not that the Virgin actually *had* intercourse (because she also had a vow of virginity) but she consented to it at the time of marriage and that, says Gratian, is what constituted the marriage.

So once again, an extraordinarily influential author had endorsed the position, even on the basis of the toughest possible case, that the essence of marriage consists not in its personalist but in its procreational aspects.

3. *Duns Scotus* (circa 1300). The Scottish Franciscan, John Duns Scotus, in his commentary on the *Sentences* of Peter Lombard, could hardly have been more explicit or more direct in lending his support to the Augustinian position. He defined marriage itself, the contract of marriage and the sacrament of marriage as follows:

> Marriage is an indissoluble bond between man and woman arising from the mutual transferral of power over each other's body for the procreation and right education of offspring.

> The contract of marriage is the mutual transferral by man and woman of their bodies for perpetual use in the procreation and right education of offspring.

> The sacrament of marriage is the expression of certain words of man and woman, signifying the mutual handing over of power over each other's body for the right procreation of offspring, efficaciously signifying by divine institution the conferral of a grace which is beneficial to each of the contractants for their mutual joining of souls.[7]

4. *Wernz* (1904). In the years just prior to the 1917 code, the idea that marriage consisted basically in the right to intercourse was generally accepted. The Jesuit, F. X. Wernz, reflected that acceptance when he described, in his Ius Decretalium, what pertained to the *essence,* to the *integrity* and to the *perfection* of marriage. He wrote:

> As regards the matrimonial contract, the *material object* is the persons

128

themselves while the *formal object* (i.e., the aspect under which it is viewed) is the undivided sharing of life. This sharing of life consists principally and *essentially* in the mutual, equal, exclusive and perpetual right and duty over the spouse's body for the generation and education of offspring, not for any other purposes, but always with the wife being subject to the husband who is her head. Then, in order that that essential communion attain its *integrity,* the communion of bed and board is necessary but can sometimes be absent without detracting from the essence of marriage. Finally, the *union of souls* through the mutual love of the spouses, although it is a condition for a happy marriage, nevertheless is not part of the *object of the matrimonial contract,* nor indeed, could the *marriage bond* consist in so fickle an element.[8]

5.   *The 1917 Code.* Given the fact that Wernz was reflecting what, by that time, was the common opinion, the actual wording of the pertinent canons in the 1917 code came as no surprise. Canon 1013 referred to the procreation and education of offspring as the "primary end of marriage" and canon 1081, §2 said that "Matrimonial consent is an act of the will by which each party gives and accepts a perpetual and exclusive right over the body for those acts which are per se apt for the generation of offspring."

With the promulgation of the 1917 code the Augustinian position became "official" and dominated Catholic thought for the next several decades.

B.   *Those Favoring the* Bonum Coniugum

1.   *Roman Law* (circa 235). Although there have always been influential proponents for the position that marriage is *primarily procreational,* it is also true that there has always existed a solid tradition in favor of the other position, namely that marriage is, at least in part, *essentially personalist.*

In classical Roman law (and it is, after all, axiomatic that for many centuries, "Ecclesia vivit lege Romana"), there were two commonly accepted definitions of marriage, but neither of them even alluded to children. Both of them spoke only of the personalist aspects of marriage.

The definition in the *Digest,* attributed to Modestinus, said that "marriage is a union of a man and a woman and a partnership of the whole of life, a participation in divine and human law."[9] The definition in the *Institutes,* attributed to Ulpian, was quite similar. It said that "marriage, or matrimony, is a union of a man and a woman, involving an undivided sharing of life."[10]

Seeing marriage as primarily personalist was, therefore, firmly rooted in Roman law.

2.   *Hugh of St. Victor* (d. 1141). Although Hugh of St. Victor has been referred

to as the "second Augustine" because of his great indebtedness to the bishop of Hippo, Hugh and Augustine had quite different notions of marriage. David Fellhauer summarized Hugh's position this way. "Hugh," he said,

> distinguished between *coniugium* and *officium coniugii*. The latter remained the obligation of mankind to propagate the human race, which required sexual intercourse. But the former, simple *coniugium*, was the marital society in itself, in which carnal copula was neither required nor always to be desired. In Hugh's theory the distincton between *coniugium* and *officium coniugii* was so pronounced that marriage actually involved two acts of consent, one of the marital society of two persons who lived in a communion of hearts and minds and who loved each other (spiritually, but not necessarily sexually); the other consent was directed to sexual intercourse. These two acts of consent, *consensus coniugalis* and *consensus coitus,* ordinarily coincided. But they need not. No one was bound to engage in marital copula, at least when its exclusion was mutually agreed upon. Thus the marriage of the Blessed Virgin and St. Joseph was a complete marriage. And more, it was the perfect marriage, the ideal, in Hugh's opinion. Mary and Joseph were united in a love which was without imperfection; they entered a conjugal society of exquisite closeness and mutual care; and they did not have sexual relations.
>
> What was, then, for Hugh of St. Victor the object of matrimonial consent? It was the *coniugalis societas,* the community of conjugal life and love. The copula was not necessary; it was not even—if one wished the perfect marriage—desirable. And it did not belong to the essence of marriage.[11]

Hugh's position, it is clear, was extremely and unrealistically spiritual. It would have to be modified before gaining any sort of widespread acceptance. It was Peter Lombard who took up that work of modification.

3. *Peter Lombard* (1158). Peter Lombard completed his *Book of Sentences* in 1158, became the Archbishop of Paris the following year, and died the year after that. His *Book of Sentences* was the standard theology text book in the Middle Ages. Most of the major theologians over the next few centuries wrote commentaries on it. It postdated Gratian's *Decretum* by seventeen or eighteen years.

Peter disagreed with Gratian on the subject of marriage and he stated his disagreement directly. He took Gratian's key question "Which sort of consent constitutes marriage? Is it consent to cohabitation or to intercourse or to both?" and he gave it a different answer. Gratian, as we saw, answered the question by saying that it was consent to carnal intercourse that makes marriage. Peter's response was that "neither the consent to cohabitation nor the consent to carnal intercourse make marriage but rather the consent to the conjugal society."[12]

So the issue was clearly joined in the twelfth century. It was one giant against another: Gratian against Peter Lombard. Gratian would eventually win, but more eventually, Peter too would have his day.

4. *Thomas Aquinas* (1256). Thomas was one of the many theologians who wrote a commentary on Peter Lombard's *Book of Sentences,* and it is principally in that commentary that we find Thomas' teaching on marriage. Thomas wrote his commentary early in his career while he was lecturing in Paris on the *Sentences.* He was only about thirty years old. The *Sentences* had been written about a hundred years earlier.

When Thomas arrived at distinction 28, where Peter had posed the question (which Gratian before him had posed) about which sort of consent constitutes marriage, consent to cohabitation or to intercourse or to both, Thomas came down firmly on the side of Peter. "It seems," he said, "that the consent which makes marriage is the consent to intercourse," and then Thomas gives four reasons to support that statement. "But in fact," he says "the contrary is true. . . . The effect should respond to the cause. But consent is the cause of marriage. Since, therefore, intercourse does not constitute the essence of marriage, it seems that it is not the consent to intercourse that causes marriage. The truth of the matter is this: that the consent that makes marriage is the consent to marriage because the proper effect of the will is the thing willed. . . . Marriage, however, as noted above, is not essentially the carnal union but rather a certain association of the husband and wife."[13]

Thomas, therefore, said essentially the same thing as Peter. For Peter the consent that makes marriage is the consent to conjugal society; for Thomas it is the consent to marriage itself, but to the whole of marriage and not just the carnal part of it.

5. *Thomas Sanchez* (1605). Although Sanchez may properly be listed in this grouping of "Those Favoring the *Bonum Coniugum,*" his endorsement of this position is rather ambiguous and equivocal, and thus symbolizes the waning strength of this viewpoint. On the one hand, Sanchez defined marriage as "the undivided, persevering sharing of life so that the purpose of marriage, which is cohabitation, may be attained,"[14] but on the other hand, he spoke of "the mutual giving over of bodies" as that "in which marriage consists" and the "increase of the human race," he intimated, was "the principal end of marriage."[15]

It would seem, therefore, that Sanchez considered the *personalist* aspects of marriage, "the undivided, persevering sharing of life" as very important, almost as important as the *procreative* aspects, but not quite. And not quite essential either.

It was a sign, perhaps, that the battle was virtually over. But not the war, of course.

131

A. *General Remarks*

Let it be clear, first of all, that if the essence of marriage consists only in the right to those acts which are per se apt for the generation of offspring, then there can be only one kind of constitutional incapacity for marriage, and that is *impotence*. If, however, the essence of marriage also includes the right to an interpersonal relationship, then there is a second kind of incapacity, namely *incompetence*.[16] To this extent, at least, there is a direct connection between a society's notion of marriage and the psychological requirements for marriage.

But even beyond that, even within the narrower limits of the "incapacitas praestandi consensum" itself,[17] one would have to assume that all things being equal, the following would be a legitimate rule of thumb: *the more sophisticated a society's notion of marriage, the higher will be the psychological aptitude level demanded of the participants.*

Historically, of course, all things have *not* been equal. At certain times and in certain societies, for example, divorce has been quite acceptable while at other times and places, the damage done by divorce to the immediate and extended family and to society as a whole has been so apparent and so frightening as to make divorce almost unthinkable. Then too, there has been over the centuries a growing appreciation of how emotional disorders impair a person's ability to relate to others. Obviously factors such as these (and many others as well) will exert a strong influence on legislators in their determination of the psychological aptitude levels for marriage that would be appropriate to their own societies.

One would expect, therefore, that the rule of thumb would suffer many exceptions. And so it has. By and large, however, the rule seems to be a generally valid one. In practice, wherever marriage has been viewed as consisting essentially only in the *procreative* aspect, the psychological requirements for marriage have tended to be low; but where the essence of marriage has also included a *personalist* element, the requirements have, as a rule, been higher.

The opinions of various authors, jurists and legislators over the centuries regarding the psychological aptitude for marriage fall generally into three categories: the rationality norm, the puberty norm, and the proportionality norm.

B. *The Rationality Norm*

During most of the Church's history, the rationality norm prevailed. This meant that when a person enjoyed the use of reason, he or she was considered *capable* of marriage; when, however, a mental disorder deprived a person of the use of reason, that person was considered *incapable* of marriage.

The following are the highlights in the history of this position.

1. *Roman Law* (circa 230). Although Roman Law saw marriage as essentially interpersonalist, its knowledge of mental disorders was quite limited and, largely as a result of that, Roman Law settled on the rationality norm and apparently found it adequate. Among the Romans a person, it seems, was either sane or insane, i.e., mad or "furious," as they said. Sane people possessed the use of reason and could marry. "Furious" people could not. The rule was stated succinctly in what eventually became an axiom, usually attributed to the jurist Paulus. It read "Neque furiosus neque furiosa matrimonium contrahere possunt sed contractum matrimonium furore non tollitur";[18] i.e., "Neither the insane man nor the insane woman can enter marriage but once the marriage is contracted, it is not invalidated by subsequent insanity."

   The axiom itself did not appear in the *Corpus Iuris Civilis* but the clear and exact sense of it was stated in slightly different words in the *Digest,*[19] and it is quite apparent that that was the only rule the Romans had to regulate psychological aptitude for marriage.

   Given their total culture it appears to have been sufficient.

2. *Gratian* (1140). Gratian's theory, as we have seen above, was that marriage is constituted by the consent of the parties to intercourse. He obviously found the "Neque furiosus" axiom quite compatible with this theory and so, in treating of the psychological requirements for marriage, Gratian simply quoted the ancient axiom (more or less) without explanation of any kind.[20] Gratian too, in other words, found it sufficient.

   In quoting the axiom, incidentally, Gratian, like Burchard of Worms before him,[21] took the liberty of ascribing it to Pope Fabian, a contemporary of Paulus, rather than to Paulus himself. Gratian did this, no doubt, because it better suited his grand purpose of exalting clergy over laity, but according to Daniel J. Boorstin, such a practice was quite acceptable in the Middle Ages. The age of modern historical criticism had not yet arrived and so certain liberties were apparently still permissible. Boorstin writes "Forgery was a prosperous medieval art. . . . Forgery of documents to support an acknowledged authority was generally considered an act of piety or patriotism. Before falsifying historical documents could have the opprobrium of forgery, it was necessary to believe that the historical past was not a flimsy fabric of myth and legend but had a solid definable reality."[22]

   Gratian, at any rate, agreed with the third century axiom and found it sufficient. Unless a person were violently insane, he or she was capable of marriage.

3. *Innocent III* (1205). In the year 1205, Pope Innocent III issued the decree *Dilectus*[23] in which he said that, if it was really true, as Rufina and her father claimed in the case at hand, that Rufina's husband, Opizo, "suffered from a

continuing madness—*continuo furore laborat"*, then clearly "a legitimate consent could not occur—*legitimus non potuerit intervenire consensus"* and the couple could separate.

This decision of Pope Innocent is one of the few examples we have over a period of many centuries of an allegation of marriage nullity on the grounds of defect of consent due to a mental disorder. Innocent, like his predecessors, used the simple rationality test.

4. *Thomas Sanchez* (1605). Not surprisingly, the position of Sanchez on this point is not entirely clear. As he was ambiguous regarding the essence of marriage, he is likewise ambiguous regarding the psychological requirements for marriage. On the one hand, Sanchez has long been considered not just a proponent but indeed the *chief* proponent of the simple rationality norm; on the other hand there are certain indications in his writing that he was more inclined towards the puberty norm. It is unclear, for example, whether Sanchez was distinguishing between deliberation and discretion. It is also unclear whether he was applying the rationality norm just to betrothal or to marriage as well. William Van Ommeren discussed the matter at considerable length in his 1961 dissertation.[24]

It is all quite confusing; but the fact is that, deservedly or not, the name of Thomas Sanchez has always been associated with the simple rationality test.

5. *Buratti* (1624). In his book, *Power to Dissolve,* John T. Noonan, Jr. indicates that, very likely, no marriage sanity case had been presented to the Roman Curia between 1205 (when Innocent III issued his *Dilectus* in the case of Rufina vs. Opizo) and 1763 (when the Sacred Congregation of the Council, as we shall see under number 6, took up the case of Jose and Ana).[25] Van Ommeren, however, does mention one case heard before the Rota in 1624 in which the ponens, Buratti, lent his full support to the simple rationality norm by writing "The madman, the captive in mind and the person destitute of senses are unable to contract marriage if, being entirely deprived of reason or sense, they suffer from permanent insanity or from a defect of sense."[26]

Buratti's wording was extremely cautious, as though to close off any possibility of moving beyond the simple rationality test. For Buratti, it seems, only the absolute madman was incapable of marriage.

6. *Sacred Congregation of the Council* (1763). In the chapter entitled "Captive in Mind," Noonan discusses the case of Jose Ponce de Leon vs. Ana Guzman heard before the S.C.C. in 1763. The marriage of Jose and Ana had actually taken place in 1728 when Ana was 22 years old. There was a great deal of evidence pointing to Ana's insanity. One witness, a stranger to Ana, testified that about a year before the wedding Ana had suddenly approached him, and, with shrill cries and laughs, told him that the devil would carry him off. Just prior to the wedding,

rumors reached Jose's family that Ana "was crazy, had always been crazy and at the present was without improvement." On the wedding night, Ana totally surprised Jose by announcing that she had made a vow of virginity and could not have sex with him. During the months following the wedding, Ana indulged in all sorts of bizarre behavior, including screaming obscenities, running naked in the sight of the household and, while naked, making piles of snow in the garden.

The decision of the S.C.C. was "non constat." The nullity of the marriage had not been proved since Ana might have been enjoying the use of reason at the moment she exchanged consent.[27]

Even within the limits of the rationality norm, this was an extremely narrow reading.

7. *Parrillo* (1928). The simple rationality test seems archaic and medieval to us today but it was vigorously defended, as recently as 1928 by Franciscus Parrillo, the rotal auditor. In a long, thirteen page law section of a negative sentence dated February 16, 1928, Parrillo argued the position in a way that was remarkably similar to the S.C.C. decision of 165 years earlier.[28] The simple rationality test was not dead yet.

C. *The Puberty Norm*

The puberty norm was proposed fairly early on but for many years failed to gain the kind of widespread practical acceptance that the simple rationality norm did, despite the immense authority of its principal proponent, namely:

1. *Thomas Aquinas* (1256). In his commentary on Peter Lombard's *Book of Sentences,* Thomas was crystal clear in stating his position regarding the degree of psychological strength required for various actions, including the entering of marriage.

He divided a person's early life into three seven year periods and then said:

> Before the end of the first septennium people are not capable of entering any sort of contract, but at the end of that first septennium they begin to be capable of promising certain things in the future, particularly those things to which natural reason more inclines them, but not of obliging themselves to a perpetual bond since they do not have a firm will; and therefore people are able to contract engagements. But at the end of the second septennium people can oblige themselves to those things which pertain to their own person like entering either religion or marriage. And after the third septennium they can even oblige themselves to those matters that concern other people as well, and after the age of twenty-five people are empowered, in accordance with the law, of disposing of their own belongings.[29]

Thomas' position that marriage involves obligations that pertain only to one's own person and not to others, seems puzzling to us now. But puzzling or not, the position of Thomas was at least firm and clear: the maturity of at least a fourteen year old was required for entering marriage.

2. *Schmalzgrueber* (1719). Among the Romans it was understood that a young person should have reached the age of puberty before marrying,[30] and this norm, which had been generally accepted by the Church, eventually found its way into the Decretals of Gregory IX.[31]

Initially the point of requiring puberty for marriage was, of course, that marriage essentially involved intercourse and it is at the age of puberty that one becomes reasonably capable of procreative intercourse.

Schmalzgrueber, however, noted that there were two reasons for requiring puberty as a minimum age for marriage:

a. Because marriage induces a greater and firmer obligation than does engagement; and consequently it demands a greater maturity of judgment and a greater freedom of consent.

b. It has been said that the use of reason is sufficient, and that the use of reason is generally present at the end of the seventh year; for marriage, however, besides the use of reason, there is also required the power of generating, that is to say, the capacity for perfect carnal intercourse.[32]

For Schmalzgrueber, therefore, the degree of discretion usually attained around the age of puberty was required in order to enter marriage.

3. *Wernz* (1904). Like Schmalzgrueber, Wernz in his pre-code commentary discussed the degree of discretion required for marriage under the general heading of the age required for marriage. He wrote:

> The canonical impediment of age in celebrating marriage is a double defect, namely the defect of discretion of judgment for conjugal consent and the defect of actual potency for generating.[33]

Wernz then went on to observe that the discretion of intellect sufficient for a valid and licit marriage is presumed present in the boy of fourteen and the girl of twelve.

Wernz, therefore, clearly endorsed the puberty norm, which meant logically that if a person were deprived by a mental disorder of *that* degree of discretion at the time of marriage, the marriage would be null.

D. *The Proportionality Norm*

1. *Gasparri* (1891). Gasparri wrote the first edition of his treatise on marriage

more than a decade before Wernz. Like Wernz, Gasparri too treated the matter of discretion under the impediment of nonage. Unlike Wernz, however, Gasparri broke new ground. He went off in a new direction. He left behind the old puberty norm and demanded instead what he called "due discretion—debita discretio," i.e., a degree of discretion that would be proportionate to marriage and which would require in the contractant a sufficient understanding of the nature, importance and essential qualities of marriage.[34]

Gasparri's new direction must have seemed, at the time, fairly insignificant. In practice, after all, there was probably little difference between the degree of discretion enjoyed by the ordinary fourteen year old and the degree of discretion proportionate to Gasparri's idea of marriage (which essentially involved only the joining of bodies). Within seventy-five years, however, Gasparri's idea of marriage would be supplanted by Vatican II's idea of marriage (which included the joining of souls), and the degree of discretion proportionate to that sort of marriage would be far greater than Gasparri or any of his contemporaries even imagined.

2. *Sincero* (1911). In a rotal decision dated August 28, 1911, Luigi Sincero endorsed Gasparri's idea of due discretion (though Sincero did not consider it germane in the case at bar) and thereby contributed to the dissemination and acceptance of the Gasparri position.[35]

3. *Prior* (1919). In a rotal decision of November 14, 1919, Prior rejected the Sanchez rule, as he called it (the simple rationality norm), noted that Thomas Aquinas demanded more than Sanchez (the puberty norm), and then himself went on to quote and endorse the Gasparri position (the proportionality norm).[36]

After Prior, more and more jurists came to accept the proportionality theory as appropriate and reasonable. As long, however, as the object of the proportionality was marriage seen as a procreative union only, the potential of the theory was severely limited. Only if marriage could be seen as both procreative and personalist would the theory be able really to expand and blossom.

To do that, however, it would take an ecumenical council.

IV. THE SECOND VATICAN COUNCIL

The Pastoral Constitution on the Church in the Modern World, *Gaudium et spes,* was promulgated by Pope Paul VI on December 7, 1965.

The Constitution saw marriage as consisting essentially of both a procreative and a personalist element; both the *bonum prolis* and the *bonum coniugum,* it said, are at the heart of marriage. The council, in other words, rejected the position of Gratian that had been dominating Catholic thought for so long and embraced instead the position of Peter Lombard.

In number 48 of the constitution, for example, we read:

> The intimate community of life and conjugal love, which has been established by the Creator and endowed by him with its own proper laws, is rooted in the covenant of its partners, that is, in their irrevocable personal consent. Therefore the institute of marriage, made firm by divine law, arises, even in the eyes of society, by that human act by which the spouses mutually hand over themselves and receive the other; once entered, however, for the sake of both the *bonum coniugum* and the *bonum prolis,* as well as of society itself, the sacred bond no longer depends on human decision alone.[37]

And number 50 concludes with these words:

> But marriage is not merely for the procreation of children: its nature as an indissoluble covenant between two people and the *bonum prolis* demand that the mutual love of the partners be properly shown, that it should grow and mature. Even in cases where, despite the intense desire of the spouses, there are no children, the marriage still perdures as a sharing and communion of the whole of life and remains valid and indissoluble.[38]

The general tenor of the constitution regarding marriage is well known. In 1965 it was a call to the whole Church to rethink what had become its accustomed position regarding the essence of marriage. The essence of marriage, said the constitution, consists not just in a procreative element but in a personalist element as well.

Besides this fundamental point, however, two other, rather incidental matters deserve mention.

First I suspect that it is not entirely accidental that the very council which promoted collegiality (i.e., decentralization) is also the council which promoted *personalism* in marriage, whereas Gratian, whose goal was to strengthen the papal hand (i.e., centralization), promoted *procreationism* in marriage. There is a certain sense, in other words, in which the more monarchical type governments tend to emphasize the *institution* (where procreation is a prime virtue) whereas the more democratic type governments favor the *individual* (where personalism is stressed). This, however, is more a sociological than a canonical question.

A second point is this. It is well known that many churchmen, including even some bishops who participated in the Second Vatican Council, vigorously resisted applying *the teaching of the council* on marriage to *the canon law* on marriage. The remarks of the council, they said, were pastoral in nature and were never meant to be uprooted and transplanted into a legal or juridical setting. To do so would be to do them violence and would come to no good.

History, however, has never been tolerant of such compartmentalization, and before long the inevitable began to happen. Beginning with Lucien Anné's decision of February 25, 1969, there were over the next fifteen years a host of decisions by the Rota and other courts around the world, directly translating the conciliar teaching into jurisprudence. The Commission for the Revision of the Code was, meanwhile, taking the same tack. Father Peter Huizing, the chairman of the Marriage Committee, reported in the 1971:I issue of *Communicationes:*

> As regards the question of how the personal relationship of the spouses along with the ordering of marriage to procreation should be expressed . . . to accord with the Second Vatican Council's description in the Pastoral Constitution on the Church in the Modern World, *Gaudium et spes,* the majority of the committee finally agreed in affirming the nature of marriage as an intimate joining of the whole of life between a man and a woman which, by its nature, is ordered to the procreation and education of offspring. Following the same constitution, the committee decided that the notion of the primary . . . and secondary ends [of marriage] . . . should no longer be used.[39]

So the stage was now set for the drafting of a new Code of Canon Law.

V. THE CODE OF CANON LAW

A. *On Marriage*

Once the committee agreed to the general philosophy as reported by Huizing, the task was then to incarnate that philosophy in appropriate canons.

This was accomplished particularly in the following areas.

1. *Nature of Marriage.* Canon 1055 of the new code (the opening canon on marriage) notes that marriage is, by its nature, ordered to both the *bonum coniugum* and the *bonum prolis.* Interestingly, the *bonum coniugum* is listed first. The same canon refers to marriage as a "partnership of the whole of life," and notes that it is entered by means of a "covenant." The opening canon on marriage of the old code (c. 1012), used the word "contract" rather than "covenant" and offered no description of marriage whatsoever.

2. *Ends of Marriage.* The second canon on marriage in the old code (c. 1013, §1) listed the procreation and education of offspring as the primary end or purpose of marriage. The new code simply omits a comparable canon.

3. *Object of Consent.* Canon 1057, §2 of the new code states that matrimonial consent is an act of the will by which a man and a woman, through an irrevocable covenant, mutually give and accept each other. The parallel canon in the old code (c. 1081, §2) described matrimonial consent as an act of the will by which each party hands over and receives the perpetual and exclusive right to the body for those acts which are per se apt for the generation of offspring.

4. *Ignorance.* Canon 1096, §1 of the new code says that for matrimonial consent to be valid, it is necessary that the contracting parties at least not be ignorant that marriage is a permanent consortium.[40] The parallel canon in the old code (c. 1082, §1) required that the contractants recognize marriage not as a consortium but simply as a society.

5. *Effects of Marriage.* Canon 1135 of the new code notes that each of the spouses has equal obligations and rights to those things which pertain to the partnership of conjugal life. The parallel canon in the old code (c. 1111) referred, instead, to the rights and obligations of the spouses "for those acts which are proper to conjugal life."

All five of these examples, especially when seen in constellation, clearly demonstrate that the vision of marriage held up by the Fathers of the Second Vatican Council has been effectively incorporated into our present Code of Canon Law.

B. *On the Psychic Requirements for Marriage*

The 1917 code contained no canon that required any particular degree of maturity or psychic health for a person to enter marriage. There was, of course, a canon on the impediment of nonage (c. 1067) and also the canon on ignorance just mentioned (c. 1082), but the old code contained no canon that stated any sort of minimum psychological aptitude required for marriage. As late as 1928, as we saw, one rotal auditor was still applying the old simple rationality test.

In accordance, however, with the rule of thumb mentioned above under III, A, that the more sophisticated a society's notion of marriage the higher will be the psychological aptitude level demanded of the participants, it was clear by 1970 that it would be absolutely imperative for the new code to contain such a canon.

That canon, as eventually promulgated, is canon 1095 and reads as follows:

Canon 1095 — They are incapable of contracting marriage:

1° who lack the sufficient use of reason;

2° who suffer from grave lack of discretion of judgment concerning essential matrimonial rights and duties which are to be mutually given and accepted;

3° who are not capable of assuming the essential obligations of matrimony due to causes of a psychic nature.

In *Annulments* and *Decisions* I have referred to the three numbers of the canon as (1°) lack of due reason, (2°) lack of due discretion, and (3°) lack of due competence. Each number deserves a brief comment here.

1. *Lack of Due Reason.* The tripartite division found in canon 1095 had actually been devised very early on. In the 1971:I issue of *Communicationes,* Father Huizing reported that in its early discussions the Marriage Committee had agreed on the following:

    > Although the principles regarding the incapacity for eliciting valid matrimonial consent are implicitly contained in the present law, it was considered appropriate that they be more distinctly and clearly expressed in the new law. The division would be as follows: the total incapacity of eliciting marital consent because of a mental disorder or disturbance by which the use of reason is impeded; incapacity stemming from a grave defect of discretion of judgment about the matrimonial rights and duties that are to be mutually exchanged; and the incapacity of assuming the essential obligations of marriage due to a serious psychosexual anomaly.[41]

    It is worth noting that Father Huizing referred to lack of due reason as a "total incapacity," as it truly is. It is, indeed, precisely because of this that the ground is virtually ignored by tribunals in their day-to-day practice. Courts tend to resist trying to prove the superfluous, and it is superfluous to show the "total" incapacity of 1° when 2° recognizes that, for an affirmative decision, it suffices to show the "partial" (or, at least, "the not so total") incapacity which comes from lack of due discretion.

    Despite what seems a practical tautology, however, the tripartite division has, nevertheless, found its way into law.

2. *Lack of Due Discretion.* The English word "discretion" refers to both the intellect and the will. When we say that we leave a matter to another person's discretion, we mean that it is left to both the judgment and the free choice of that person.

    The Latin word has traditionally had the same meaning. If one looks up "Discretio iudicii" in Palazzini's *Dictionarium Morale et Canonicum,* it says see "Capacitas intelligendi et volendi" and when one turns to that heading, it begins by noting that "discretio iudicii" (which is the same phrase used in 1095, 2°) consists of two elements: understanding and willing.[42]

    The meaning of discretion is, therefore, quite clear. It means first of all that a person must understand the duties that are to be assumed, and that secondly he or she freely choose to assume those understood duties.

3. *Lack of Due Competence.* The statement was made earlier (above, III, A) that when the essence of marriage was understood to consist only in the right to intercourse, then there would be only one sort of constitutional incapacity for marriage, namely the incapacity for intercourse, i.e.,

impotence. This was certainly logical and was clearly implied in the opening pages of Gasparri's work on marriage.[43]

It should be remembered, however, that the 1917 code recognized not only the *essence* of marriage (the right to intercourse) but also two *essential properties* of marriage (unity, i.e., fidelity, and indissolubility). If, therefore, it were recognized that a person could be psychologically incapable of fidelity or indissolubility, then besides *impotence* there would be a second kind of constitutional incapacity, namely *incompetence.* So understood, incompetence would, of course, have an extremely limited scope; it would apply only to people who were truly incapable of either fidelity or perpetuity, usually the former.

The concept seems to have been used for the first time by the Rota in a decision given by Alberto Canestri on February 21, 1948. At the time Canestri referred to incompetence as "moral impotence," a term which gained fairly wide acceptance for a time but was eventually discarded. Canestri wrote:

> There are men and women who, by reason of an atavistic or hereditary imperfection, or because they are mired in vice or have been poisoned by breathing in the fumes of a corrupt society, are so depraved, especially in the area of sexual desire, that they are rendered incapable of marriage by a kind of impotence, not a physical but a moral impotence.[44]

Given this background, that incompetence or moral impotence as understood from 1948 on referred primarily to an incapacity for fidelity due to hyperaesthesia, it is understandable that the 1970 draft and even the 1975 draft of canon 1095 spoke of people being incapable of assuming the obligations of marriage *due to a psycho-sexual anomaly.* Once it was realized, however, that the very essence of marriage included the right to an interpersonal relationship, then it was obvious that the phrase "due to a psycho-sexual anomaly" was unduly restrictive and the phrase was dropped. The 1980 draft changed "psycho-sexual anomaly" to "psychic anomaly," and the 1983 code spoke only of "causes of a psychic nature."

According to the present code, therefore, a marriage is rendered null by any psychological reason (even though it is not a "disorder" or "anomaly") whenever that reason or cause renders a spouse incapable of assuming the essential obligations of marriage, especially the obligation of engaging in an interpersonal relationship.

VI. CONCLUDING REMARKS

Canon 1095 of the new Code of Canon Law, taken in context, says certain things but leaves other things unsaid.

It says that in order to enter a valid marriage, a person must enjoy sufficient discretion and sufficient competence for a marital consortium.

Left unsaid, however, is the precise nature of a consortium. Also left unsaid is the meaning of "sufficient discretion" and "sufficient competence"; but it is clear that these latter terms are essentially relational to the former, so that if we knew the precise meaning of the term "consortium" then we would, at least, be well on our way to understanding how much discretion and how much competence would be "sufficient."

The special task for the jurist in our time, therefore, is to determine as precisely as possible the essential elements that go to make up a consortium. We could start, for example, with the dictionary definitions and look to the right of one spouse to the (1) company, (2) affection, and (3) help of the other. Or we could consider Ombretta Fumagalli Carulli's three "constitutive elements" of conjugal love: (1) recognizing the other as a person endowed with his or her own identity, (2) regarding the other as a person with whom one wants to establish a common life, and (3) wishing the other well.[45] My own three components of (1) self revelation, (2) understanding, and (3) loving, which were adapted from Eugene C. Kennedy's "signs of life in marriage,"[46] seem to me to be the basic practical skills one must enjoy in order to enter a stable, intimate relationship. And there are several other approaches that deserve consideration as well.[47]

Above all, perhaps, we should be reading and listening to what married men and women are saying about what it really takes to make it in marriage. Male celibates are not without their own insights into marriage but it certainly makes no sense to listen only and exclusively to them, as we have in fact done for so many years.

Canon 1095 is a useful canon but it leaves much to the "discretion," i.e. to the insightful decisions, of the judges. Not all of us, of course, will understand the canon in exactly the same way but all of us must, at least, be as knowledgeable and as equitable and as responsible and as charitable as, with God's grace, we can be.

ENDNOTES

[1] Theodore Mackin, *What is Marriage?* (New York: Paulist, 1982), p. 128.
[2] St. Augustine, *De Bono Coniugali,* c. 6; *PL* 40: 377-378.
[3] St. Augustine, *Contra Faustum Manichaeum,* lib. 19, c. 26; *PL* 42: 365.
[4] St. Augustine, *De Coniugiis Adulterinis,* lib. 2, c. 12: *PL* 40: 479.
[5] *Decretum,* C. 27, q. 2, c. 2.
[6] *Decretum,* C. 27, q. 2, c. 3.
[7] Duns Scotus, Quaestiones in quartum librum Sententiarum, dist. 26, q. unica (*Omnia opera,* Vol. 19, p. 186).
[8] Francesco Xav. Wernz, S.J., *Ius Decretalium,* Tomus IV (Romae: Typographia Polyglotta S. C. De Propaganda Fide, 1904), p. 48.
[9] *Digesta,* 23, 2, 1.
[10] *Instituta,* 1, 9, 1.
[11] David Fellhauer, "The 'Consortium Omnis Vitae' as a Juridical Element of Marriage," *Studia Canonica* 13 (1979) 58-59.
[12] Peter Lombard, *Libri IV Sententiarum,* lib. IV, dist. 28.

[13] St. Thomas, *In IV Sent,* d. 28, art. 4

[14] Thomas Sanchez, *De Sancto Matrimonii Sacramento,* lib. 2, disp. 1, n. 8.

[15] Ibid., lib. 2, disp. 4, n. 3.

[16] Lawrence G. Wrenn, *Annulments* p. 7 under B5.

[17] As opposed to incompetence, which is the "incapacitas praestandi obiectum consensus."

[18] *Fontes Iuris Ante Justiniani,* II, 345.

[19] *Digesta,* 23, 2, 16.

[20] *Decretum,* C. 32, c. 26.

[21] Burchardus, X, 28-29; *PL* 140: 819.

[22] Daniel J. Boorstin, *The Discoverers* (New York: Random House, 1983), p. 576.

[23] *X,* 4, 1, 24.

[24] William M. Van Ommeren, *Mental Illness Affecting Matrimonial Consent* (Washington: Catholic University of America Press, 1961), pp. 105-132. See also John R. Keating, *The Bearing of Mental Impairment on the Validity of Marriage* (Rome: Gregorian University Press, 1964), pp. 123-143.

[25] John T. Noonan, Jr., *Power to Dissolve* (Cambridge: The Belknap Press of Harvard University Press, 1972), pp. 154-155. "Apart from Innocent III's decision incorporated in the decretal *Dilectus,* neither the advocates of the parties nor the Secretary of the S.C.C. were able to refer to any instance of a marriage attacked for insanity before any court of the Curia. It would be rash to say that no marriage sanity case had gone to Rome since *Dilectus* had been issued in 1205, but where precedent is unknown it is as good as nonexistent."

[26] *S.R.R.D.,* coram Buratti (Rome, 1624), annot. ad decis. 763, as quoted in Van Ommeren, p. 38.

[27] Noonan, pp. 136-158.

[28] *S.R.R.D.* 20: 58-71

[29] St. Thomas, *In IV Sent.,* d. 27, q. 2, a. 2, n. 7.

[30] *Instituta* 1, 10.

[31] *X,* 4, 2-3.

[32] Franciscus Schmalzgrueber, *Ius Ecclesiasticum Universum,* tom. 4, pars 1, tit. 2. See also tom. 4, pars 1. tit. 1, n. 14.

[33] Wernz, p. 469.

[34] Gasparri, *De Matrimonio* (Paris, 1891), n. 777. In Gasparri's 1932 edition, see n. 783.

[35] *S.R.R.D.* 3: 450.

[36] *S.R.R.D.* 11: 173. See also *AAS* 13 (1921) 56.

[37] *Gaudium et spes,* no. 48.

[38] *Gaudium et spes,* no. 50.

[39] *Communicationes* 3 (1971) 70.

[40] The word "consortium" is a legitimate word in the English language but, except for this one canon, the CLSA translation has translated it "partnership." See cc. 1055, 1098 and 1135. The *American Heritage Dictionary* gives, as one of its meanings for the word consortium, "a husband's right to the company, help and affection of his wife [and] the right of the wife to the same." *Webster's New Collegiate Dictionary* defines consortium as "the legal right of one spouse to the company, affection and service of the other."

[41] *Communicationes* 3 (1971). See also *Communicationes* 7 (1975) 41 for the actual 1970 draft. Regarding Huizing's statement about the *implicit* presence of the notion of incapacity in the 1917 code, see cc. 1035 and 1081, §1.

[42] Petrus Palazzini, *Dictionarium Morale et Canonicum,* 4 vols. (Rome: Catholic Book Agency, 1962), vol. 2, p. 103 and vol. 1, p. 536.

[43] Gasparri, §7.

[44] *S.R.R.D.* 40: 64.

[45] Ombretta Fumagalli Carulli, "Essenza ed esistenza nell'amore coniugale: Considerazioni canonistiche," *Ephemerides Iuris Canonici* 36 (1980) 216-218.

[46] Eugene C. Kennedy, "Signs of Life in Marriage" in *Divorce and Remarriage in the Catholic Church,* ed. Lawrence G. Wrenn (New York: Newman Press, 1973), pp. 121-133.

[47] See, for example, *Decisions,* first edition, p. 60.

Refining The Essence Of Marriage

This paper will consist of five sections. The first section will discuss the Jemolo case, which was a hypothetical case devised some years ago to test the common understanding of marriage that prevailed at the time. The Jemolo case states the problem. The next section, "Some Preliminary Observations," consists of a half dozen points which try to keep us on the straight and narrow, and so facilitate our attempt to come up with a solution to the problem. The third section attempts to define with some reasonable degree of precision the nature and essence of the marital relationship. This section might be called "A Solution" or perhaps more realistically "Towards A Solution." In the fourth section we will discuss several possible objections to the solution proposed. And finally, some practical applications of the theory will be considered, at least briefly.

A. The Jemolo Case

Forty-five years ago the Italian jurist, A. C. Jemolo, asked his students and his readers to think hard about a hypothetical marriage case.[1] An honest pondering of the case, Jemolo implied, would necessarily involve a thorough rethinking of the then current understanding of marriage.

The case that Jemolo posed was this: a man marries a woman not primarily out of love or to have a family or for any of the usual reasons; rather he marries her primarily to carry out a vendetta. His principal interest is to be mean and cruel to his wife and to make her pay for all the injuries committed by her family against him and his family.

Is it possible, asked Jemolo, that such an arrangement could ever be considered a valid marriage? The question was, at the time, an intriguing and troublesome one. Under the old code marital consent consisted in the exchange of rights to those acts which are per se apt for the generation of offspring. If in an individual case those rights *were* exchanged, and if at the same time neither of the essential properties of marriage (unity and indissolubility) were excluded, then a valid marriage would occur.

In terms of the *bona matrimonii* (the goods or blessings of marriage), all three *bona* (the *bonum prolis,* the *bonum fidei,* and the *bonum sacramenti*) could conceivably be present in such a case. Indeed in the scenario posed by Jemolo, the man did intend to have children; he did intend to be faithful to his wife (in the minimal sense tht he was not reserving to himself the right to have a lover on the side); and he did intend to cohabit with his wife until death. The man, furthermore, was quite capable of fulfilling all those obligations.

In other words the man did, first of all, have the capacity for marriage as it was then understood, and secondly, he did not simulate marriage either totally or partially. *Technically,* therefore, he entered what would have to be regarded as a valid marriage.

Yet common sense told Jemolo that such an arrangement could not possibly be called a marriage. This kind of hate-filled vendetta was absolutely and unequivocally unworthy of being considered a marriage, let alone a *sacrament* of marriage. It is much more like a *Mafia* contract than a *marriage* contract; certainly it is not a marriage *covenant.*

The obvious implication, of course, was that if the Church judged that man's vendetta-inspired union to be a valid marriage, then there was something radically wrong with the Church's understanding of marriage. The essence of marriage needed reexamination. Something important, indeed something essential must have been overlooked and omitted. There must be something above and beyond the *bonum prolis,* the *bonum fidei,* and the *bonum sacramenti.* And that was the problem: if the marriage of the man bent on vendetta is *not* a marriage, and surely it is not, then *why* is it not? In canonical terms, what essential element was lacking in that arrangement which rendered it non-marital, that is to say, something less than a marriage?

B. Preliminary Observations

1. First I should like to point out what the missing element is *not.* The missing element is not to be found by looking at a person's *motive* for marrying. Jurisprudence has always held that an otherwise valid marriage is never rendered invalid simply by an unworthy motive. A person, for example, may marry for money or prestige, or to gain citizenship in a desirable country, or to escape from an unhappy home life, or for countless other less than noble reasons. Such motives, however, do not in themselves invalidate a marriage. Such motives can only affect validity when and if they also exclude the essence of marriage. If, for example, a Polish man married an American woman in order to gain entry into the United States, that motivation would not ordinarily invalidate the marriage. It could invalidate the marriage, if, say, the man intended to divorce the woman as soon as he obtained his citizenship, but ordinarily and of itself it would not vitiate the marriage.

   It has always been understood, in other words, that the *finis operis* (in this case the purpose of marriage itself) and the *finis operantis* (the motive of the spouse in marrying) do not necessarily have to coincide. It is probably nice if they do but they do not have to. All that is absolutely required is that the spouse, for whatever reason, consent to the essence of marriage. This is what is known as the principle of the irrelevancy of motive.

   In the Jemolo case the man's motive for marrying was, of course, immoral; but despite this, he did not exclude the essence of marriage as it was understood at the time. He consented to the three *bona* of marriage and that made the marriage valid. In other words, when we look for the missing element in the Jemolo case, we should look not at the *finis operantis* but at the *finis operis;* we should look to the essence of marriage itself.

2. My second observation flows from the first and is really the other side of the coin. It is the flip side of the principle of the irrelevancy of motive. It is this: just as generally speaking the presence of a bad motive does not result in invalidity, so it is equally true that the absence of a good motive likewise does not result in invalidity.

    This, I think, is an important point because it means that if jurisprudence were eventually to conclude that some specific element, for example *love,* is essential to marriage, then the love that would be at issue would *not* be the love that motivates people to marry. Courts would not, therefore, declare a marriage null because it had been shown that one or both of the spouses were not "in love" when they married or that they failed to marry for reasons of love. Again, motivation is basically irrelevant. Rather, the love that would be at issue would be something intrinsic to marriage itself. It would be part of the object of consent. It would be something the parties consent to.

    If, therefore, jurisprudence were eventually to conclude that love is essential to marriage then it would be expected that when people marry, they would agree—even if they were not marrying for reasons of love—that they would be loving persons to each other for the rest of their lives. If therefore love comes to be accepted as essential to marriage, this and only this will be the love we are talking about.

3. My third observation is a direct, if rather vague and quite general, response to the question raised by the Jemolo case. In the Jemolo case the man consented to the *bonum prolis,* the *bonum fidei* and the *bonum sacramenti* and therefore seemed to enter a technically valid marriage. The question is: was there another element, essential to marriage, an element to which the man did not consent, which rendered the marriage invalid? In light of the Second Vatican Council and of the 1983 code, the answer is crystal clear. The answer is that besides the three *bona* recognized prior to Vatican II, we now know that there is a fourth *bonum* which is equally essential to marriage, namely the *bonum coniugum.*

    Canon 1055, §1, the opening canon on marriage, makes this very clear. It reads: "The matrimonial covenant, by which a man and a woman establish between themselves a partnership of the whole of life, is by its nature ordered to the *bonum coniugum* and to the procreation and education of offspring. . . ."

    Common sense told us all along, of course, that this was the basic problem in the Jemolo case. The man was not intending to be his wife's *helpmate* but rather her *antagonist,* and that is what rendered his union a non-marriage. This was not so clear in 1941 as it is now. Now it is clear that there are not three essential *bona* but four. The precise, exact, detailed meaning of the *bonum coniugum* we shall try to clarify during the course of these remarks, but for the present I would simply like to make the point that the *bonum coniugum,* whatever it involves, is definitely and certainly an essential element of marriage.

4. I would note, fourthly, that, except for indissolubility, it is really inaccurate to say that the *bona matrimonii* themselves pertain to the essence of marriage. It is rather the right, the ius ad bona matrimonii, that pertains to the essence. Take the *bonum fidei,* for example. It is not really fidelity but rather the *right* to fidelity that pertains to the essence of marriage. If this were not so, if fidelity itself pertained to the essence of marriage, then part of the essence of marriage and therefore the marriage itself would cease to exist whenever a spouse was unfaithful; that, of course, is not true.

    The same is true of the *bonum coniugum.* Strictly speaking it is not the *bonum coniugum* but the right to the *bonum coniugum* exchanged at the time of the wedding that belongs to the essence of marriage. It is, therefore, the actual pledge of the spouses to contribute to their mutual welfare that is essential and constitutive of a valid marriage. If at some later time the actual, de facto *bonum coniugum* should dissipate—if, for example, the couple's love for each other should turn to hate—that disappearance of the *bonum coniugum* would not invalidate or dissolve the marriage. What is essential is not the *bonum coniugum* but rather the right to the *bonum coniugum.*

5. A fifth preliminary observation is this. The specific components of the *bonum coniugum* might differ from culture to culture. It is quite possible, for example, that conjugal love would be considered an essential component of the *bonum coniugum* in the twentieth century whereas it would not have been regarded as absolutely essential in the eighteenth century.

    This was a point made by Lucien Anné in his famous decision of February 25, 1969.[2] It strikes me as a valid and practical observation. It means, for example, that as we turn our attention to the task of determining the precise components of the *bonum coniugum,* it is not necessary that we arrive at some sort of pure, universal essence that would be applicable for all places and for all times. Rather it would suffice if we could identify with reasonable preciseness the components of the *bonum coniugum* for this time and this place, that is to say, for our own culture and our own civilization.

6. My final preliminary observation is a simple word of caution, namely that in our attempt to locate and identify the exact dimensions of the *bonum coniugum* for our culture, it is important that we avoid being either too generous or too stingy, too inclusive or too exclusive.

    The Jemolo case made it clear that the 1917 code had sinned by being too exclusive, that in excluding the *bonum coniugum* from the essence of marriage it had artificially truncated the notion of marriage and deprived it of some of its essential richness. The canonists of the early twentieth century fell into a trap regarding the essence of marriage. Now that that error has been corrected we do not want to fall into a similar trap, this time regarding the essence not of marriage itself but of the *bonum coniugum*. On the one hand we *do not want to say*, "Yes, the bonum coniugum is essential but the *bonum coniugum* means only that the spouses should be civil to each other." On the other hand, neither do we want to say, "The *bonum coniugum* is essential and that means that the spouses must be madly in love with each other or there is no marriage." These two extremes must be avoided. The challenge will be to find the truth, which will not necessarily be exactly in the middle but should, at least, be somewhere between the two extremes.

C. Towards A Solution

Over the years jurisprudence has defined with reasonable precision the sense of the three traditional *bona*. The *bonum prolis* refers to the right of the parties to non-contraceptive intercourse; the *bonum fidei* refers to the right of the parties to be their spouse's only sex partner; the *bonum sacramenti* refers to the indissolubility of marriage.

The essence of the fourth *bonum*, the *bonum coniugum*, however, is not yet so clear. Does it refer to the right of the parties to simple, basic goodwill from their spouse? Or does it go so far as to include a right to a romantic, passionate love?

As with the other *bona*, a clarification of this issue will come gradually through the work of jurisprudence. But in this section of the paper I would like to discuss six of the more obvious qualities that might constitute the essence of the *bonum coniugum*. They are partnership, benevolence, companionship, friendship, caring, and finally love.

1. *Partnership*

Since marriage is a consortium and the usual translation of "consortium" is partnership, and since canon 1135 says that "each of the spouses has equal obligations and rights to those things which pertain to the partnership of conjugal life," it might seem that that quality of partnership constitutes the nucleus of the *bonum coniugum*.

Justice Story defined a partnership as "a relation existing between two or more competent persons who have contracted to place their money, effects, labor and skill, or some or all of them, in lawful commerce or business with the understanding that there shall be a communion of profit among them." In a more general sense a partner is anyone who has a part in something. A partner is a partaker, a sharer, a participant, an associate, or a colleague.

In light of all this it is clear, I think, that partnership is a pretty impersonal, business-like arrangement. Still there is something to be said for it. In terms of the Jemolo case one would be hard pressed to say that the man in that case recognized the woman as a true partner. On the contrary, he treated her not as a partner but as a victim. Certainly he did not intend her to share in what Justice Story called the "communion of profit among them." So even if jurisprudence had, in those days, recognized that much, namely that the essence of marriage required a true partnership, then the union proposed by Jemolo could easily have been declared null according to the then accepted rules of jurisprudence.

Mere partnership would therefore seem to have solved the Jemolo case. But that was forty-five years ago and since then the question has shifted somewhat. What we want to know now is whether it can be said that partnership is the special quality that constitutes the nucleus of the *bonum coniugum*. The answer, I think, is no. Since the Second Vatican Council, it seems to me, mainstream jurisprudence has concluded that mere partnership, that is, merely being a colleague, is not enough; some interpersonal relationship is required as constitutive of the essential nucleus of the *bonum coniugum*. Mere partnership therefore is too impersonal and too business-like to qualify even as the bare minimum that would be required for a valid marriage.

2. *Benevolence*

Benevolence, otherwise known as goodwill, seems to suffer from the same basic defect as partnership: it is too impersonal to constitute the essence of marriage. Marriage is now recognized as being an interpersonal relationship of some depth and intensity. But this is not what benevolence is.

Benevolence is defined in Webster's as the "kindly disposition to do good and promote the welfare of others: goodwill." Given that definition it would seem that the people who would appropriately exercise benevolence would be, not husband and wife toward each other, but rather benefactors and philanthropists toward their beneficiaries. Benevolence, I take it, can be present and even practiced without even knowing who the beneficiary is. It seems evident, therefore, that mere benevolence or goodwill would necessarily fall far short of what is required in order to have a true *bonum coniugum*. It is not enough, in other words, for husbands and wives to treat each other as beneficiaries. Some degree of personalism is absolutely essential in marriage.

Thomas Aquinas, incidentally, made a clear distinction between love on the one hand and goodwill or benevolence on the other. Love, he said, involves much more than simply wishing a person well. Goodwill, he said, is neither friendship nor love but just the beginning, just the first step or groundwork of friendship, the *principium amicitiae*.[3]

One would of course expect spouses to exercise goodwill toward each other, but one would also expect more. Mere benevolence is not enough to constitute a real marriage.

3. *Companionship*

Companionship is more personal than benevolence and to that extent is closer to what might constitute the nucleus of the *bonum coniugum*. The word "companion" comes from "cum" and "panis". A companion, therefore, is one with whom you break bread. He or she is not some nameless beneficiary of your kindness but rather an acquaintance with whom you spend time and share experiences on the great journey of life.

C. S. Lewis suggests that companionship is a product of the gregarious instinct in human nature, and notes that it might also be called "clubbableness" since companionship is the kind of thing shared by men and women at the golf club or even in the barroom.[4] Companionship, however, is something less than friendship. It is, you might say, the matrix of friendship in that given the right people and a shared interest, friendship might grow and develop out of it. But companionship is not so rich or so deep as friendship. Friendship is gold; companionship is silver.

But the jurisprudential question is whether the *bonum coniugum* could be said to be present if, at the time of the wedding, the spouses consented not to love one another or even to be friends, but simply to be companions. The famous decision of November 29, 1975 of the five Signatura judges in the Utrecht case answered in the affirmative.[5] In the opinion of those judges *communio vitae* meant nothing more than the *communio thori, mensae et habitationis* of the old canon 1128. In that view, in other words, a spouse was precisely a companion, or more precisely a sexual companion, that is to say, one with whom the other party broke bread and had sex, one with whom bed and board were shared.

Since that time, however, mainstream jurisprudence has, I think, come to require more than that. The present view is that spouses must share not just bed and board but they must share their whole lives as well. Marriage is a *consortium totius vitae,* as canon 1055 says. It is a sharing not just of externals but of the internal lives of the spouses as well, a sharing of their thoughts and feelings and, in some way, of their very selves.

Mere companionship, therefore, is not enough to constitute the *bonum coniugum.*

4. *Friendship*

St. Thomas says that there are five things that pertain to friendship: we should wish our friends well (benevolence); we should wish them to be and to live; we should take pleasure in their company (companionship); we should make choice of the same things; and we should grieve and rejoice with them.[6]

Clearly for Thomas friendship includes such things as benevolence and companionship, but it is also something over and above those things and is distinct from both of them. Friendship, furthermore, is likewise distinct from love, at least from the love of lovers. C. S. Lewis notes the following differences between friendship and love. First, lovers are always talking to each other about their love, whereas friends hardly ever talk to one another about their friendship. Second, lovers are normally face to face, absorbed in each other, whereas friends tend to stand side by side, absorbed in some common interest. Third, love is an exclusive relationship between two people only, whereas in friendship two friends delight to be joined by a third, and three by a fourth. "True friendship," says Lewis, "is the least jealous of loves."[7]

So once again we come to the jurisprudential question: what is it that constitutes the essence of the *bonum coniugum?* Is it enough if the spouses pledge to be each other's lifelong friend, even each other's *best* friend forever?

Friendship, as we noted, is golden. It is a wonderful, noble thing and has been extolled by many of history's greatest poets and philosophers. But in spite of that, the right to friendship, it seems to me, still falls short of what is necessary for a valid marital relationship, principally because the marital relationship must have a certain exclusive quality about it whereas friendship, by definition, is not exclusive but inclusive.

Spouses should certainly be friends, just as they should be benevolent partners and companions. But none of those qualities, taken either separately or together, is sufficient to constitute the essential nucleus of the *bonum coniugum.* For that something more is required.

5. *Caring*

The verb "to care" has many meanings. It is, first of all, often used as a synonym for love. Morton T. Kelsey, for example, has written a book which has as its title *Caring,* but as its subtitle, *How Can We Love One Another?* In fact, this book entitled *Caring* is really all about *loving.* Second, caring can denote a burdensome sense of responsibility and solicitude, or trouble caused by duties, and in that sense we speak of a "careworn face." Third, it can mean to have charge of or to be responsible for, as a doctor or nurse cares for a patient and a shepherd or pastor cares for the flock. In this sense it is the opposite of apathy.

The classic, popular discussion of the subject is in a little book called *On Caring* written by Milton Mayeroff. Mayeroff, in effect, adopts the third meaning of the term, namely to be responsible for something or someone. More precisely, Mayeroff defines caring as "helping the other grow,"[8] which is basically what the doctor, nurse, shepherd and pastor do. Rollo May, in his book *Love and Will,* adopts this same meaning of the term. May writes, "If I care about being, I will shepherd it with some attention paid to its welfare."[9]

Seeing care as "helping the other grow" is, in fact, a very ancient way of viewing care. Martin Heidegger recounts this ancient parable in which care is portrayed as a shaper and molder of the human being, or to use Mayeroff's expression, as one who helps another grow:

> Once when "Care" was crossing a river, she saw some clay; she thoughtfully took up a piece and began to shape it. While she was meditating on what she had made, Jupiter came by. "Care" asked him to give it spirit, and this he gladly granted. But when she wanted her name to be bestowed upon it, he forbade this, and demanded that it be given his name instead. While "Care" and Jupiter were disputing, Earth arose and desired that her own name be conferred on the creature, since she had furnished it with part of her body. They asked Saturn to be their arbiter, and he made the following decision, which seemed a just one: "Since you, Jupiter, have given its spirit, you shall receive that spirit at its death; and since you, Earth, have given its body, you shall receive its body. But since 'Care' first shaped this creature, she shall possess it as long as it lives. And because there is now a dispute among you as to its name, let it be called homo, for it is made out of humus (earth)."[10]

In saying that care "shall possess it as long as it lives," this ancient parable implies that the human being is essentially and irrevocably constituted as a caring person. This is certainly an upbeat, optimistic anthropology that suggests that our common vocation as human beings is to help one another grow. We are all called to care for one another. Caring is seen, therefore, as a kind of primordial human disposition.

But having said that, let us return once again to the jurisprudential question. In order to exchange the right to the bonum coniugum what precisely is it that the spouses pledge to do? Is it that they pledge themselves to be caring spouses to each other?

I think it is not, and the reason I think it is not is this. In order to bring about the bonum coniugum it is essential that the spouses not only care for each other, that is, help each other grow; it is also necessary that they allow themselves to be cared for. Caring, in other words, is only half the process. In the helping professions and in many other situations as well, caring alone works fine and can be a beautiful thing. But in close interpersonal relationships including marriage, caring alone (without a corresponding openness to be cared for) can be destructive.

Woody Allen's movie Hannah And Her Sisters is, I think, a clear illustration of this. Hannah And Her Sisters, as the title implies, is about the relationship of Hannah (played by Mia Farrow) with her two sisters, Lee and Holly. But it is also about Hannah's relationship with her two husbands, her first husband being Woody Allen, her second Michael Caine.

Hannah is a charming, efficient, accomplished, caring, thoughtful, considerate, self-sufficient, wonderful person. She has given up a career on the stage in order to have a family but in the course of the movie returns to do a single play on Broadway for which she gets rave reviews. She also deserves rave reviews as a homemaker and mother and she is, in general, a marvelous person, totally in control of her own life and always willing to help others.

The only problem is that she somehow manages to undermine everybody around her. Hannah and her first husband, Woody Allen, (as we see in flashbacks) are unable to have children and when they go to a doctor in an attempt to remedy the situation they find that Woody is incurably sterile. Hannah's second husband, Michael Caine, is deeply in love with Hannah. But at one point he says to her "It's impossible to live with someone like you, who is so giving but who has no needs of her own," and he goes out and has an affair with Hannah's sister Lee. Lee is a good person but is so overwhelmed by Hannah's flawlessness that she first lives with a totally antisocial, intellectual artist, and then has her fling with Michael Caine. Then there is Holly who, like Lee, is overpowered by Hannah and becomes a drug addict and can never figure out what she wants to do with her life. Interestingly, though, before the movie ends, Holly marries Woody Allen and, lo and behold, she becomes pregnant by Woody who, when he was with Hannah, was regarded as incurably sterile.

The message, I think, is clear; namely, in close interpersonal relationships, caring alone is not enough. Unless, indeed, it is coupled with a willingness to be cared for, caring alone can be a destructive and sterilizing thing in an institution like marriage. When, however, caring is in fact coupled with an openness to being cared for, then it is no longer called caring but something else, namely love.

6.   Love

Love, as we know, is a many splendored thing; but in our context, at least, it may be defined as an affective tendency toward another person which is dialogical in nature and which involves union with the other.

To descibe love as an "affective tendency" is to distinguish it immediately from infatuation. A tendency is just an inclination or a propensity, and connotes perhaps a strong and eager but nevertheless a somewhat gentle movement, whereas infatuation involves a kind of dizzy, careening, uncontrolled, raging flame of desire. Etymologically the word infatuation comes from the Latin *fatuitas*, which means "foolishness"; love, on the other hand, is the most unfoolish thing in the world.

The phrase "affective tendency" also distinguishes love itself or simple love from romantic love. In her book *The Theology of Romantic Love, A Study in the Writings of Charles Williams*, Mary McDermott Shideler notes that romantic love always begins with the shock of an intense personal experience and then causes the lover, both in body and mind, to function as a whole person, as an integrated entity, focusing all his or her powers on the beloved. It is the kind of love that Dante had for Beatrice and, in our century, the kind of love that Wally Simpson and King Edward VIII seem to have had for each other. But as Shideler points out, that kind of romantic, heroic love is not the only love. "Sweetness and serenity," she says, "quiet affection and gradual development, belong as truly to the Kingdom of Love as do the tumults of the romantic encounter. The absence of the romantic response to experience implies no disparagement, because this can be a difference in style of loving, rather than a difference in degree or depth of love."[11]

Finally, the term "affective tendency" also distinguishes love from a completely cooled down, business-like experience that pertains only to the mind and the reasoning faculty. Love is affective. It involves the heart and the emotions. St. Thomas treats of love under the heading of the soul's passions[12] along with hatred, desire and aversion, joy and sorrow, hope and despair, fear and daring, and anger. Love, said St. Thomas, pertains to the appetite,[13] is rightly classified as a passion,[14] can easily lead to ecstasy,[15] and involves a "union of affection, without which," he says "there is no love."[16]

Love, therefore, is neither infatuation nor romantic love on the one hand, nor is it a kind of intellectual esteem or respect on the other. It is rather an affective tendency.

The second part of the definition of love notes that is is dialogical in nature. Unlike caring, therefore, which in itself is a kind of monologue, love is seen rather as a conversation, a dialogue. It involves two axes or poles in each person around which the love flows.

These two poles were called by Aquinas *amor concupiscentiae* and *amor benevolentiae,*[17] which Karl Rahner translates respectively as love of desire and love of generosity.[18] Love of desire, as the term implies, involves desiring the other as a source of legitimate self-fulfillment, whereas love of generosity involves wanting the best for one's beloved for the beloved's own sake. In all healthy human love, however, both poles coexist and are more or less constantly active. In all healthy human love there must be both giving and receiving. Love is essentially an exchange. Contrary to the axiom, the fact is that it is not always more blessed to give than to receive.[19] Human love, at any rate, cannot exist without both.

Finally let me mention briefly the third element in the definition of love, namely that it involves union with the other. Thomas devotes a separate article to this, noting that every love is a unitive force and that both poles, the love of desire and the love of generosity, are each in its own way creative of a unity between the lover and the beloved. Love is always a bonding force that makes for communion and, in some sense at least, makes two people one.[20]

If one were to list reasons in favor of the position that the essence of the *bonum coniugum* consists in the *ius ad amorem,* this perhaps would be the first, namely that both marriage and love have the same effect. They both create a bond between people; in both cases, the two people become one. In marriage they become one *flesh* which is not necessarily true in all love. But this, I think, is the point. Whereas it is all right for two people to become one without being one flesh, it is not all right for two people to become one flesh without their first having become one. It is all right, in other words, for two people to love each other without being lovers, but it is not all right for people to become lovers unless they love each other. In marriage the spouses have a right to have intercourse, but there is something wrong (and probably immoral) if they have intercourse without loving each other.

This is the fundamental reason why the *bonum prolis* and the *bonum coniugum* go hand in hand and are inseparable: because the essence of the *bonum coniugum* is the *ius ad amorem,* and unless that is present it is not right to have intercourse. It perhaps even explains why in canon 1055, §1, the *bonum coniugum* is mentioned first and the *bonum prolis* second: because people should commit themselves to loving each other before they make love.

A second reason in support of the essentiality of the *ius ad amorem* is the importance assigned to love in papal encyclicals, notably *Casti connubii* (n. 23) and *Humanae vitae* (nn. 8-9). In the former Pius XI referred to love as that "excellent soil" in which conjugal faith has rooted and he noted that "love of husband and wife . . . pervades all the duties of married life and holds pride of place in Christian marriage." In the latter Paul VI noted that marital love was part of God's loving design, and that its characteristic features are that it be fully human, total, faithful, exclusive and fruitful.

A third reason for saying that the *bonum coniugum* consists in the parties pledging to be loving persons to each other is found in the Second Vatican Council's *Gaudium et spes* (nn. 48-50) which assigns to love an absolutely central and pervasive role in marriage, and which describes marriage as "an intimate community of life and love."

A fourth reason is the one developed by Theodore Mackin. He points out that if love is not essential to marriage, then the sacrament of matrimony is lacking a matrix.[21] St. Paul pointed out in the fifth chapter of Ephesians that the love of wife and husband in marriage is the symbol of the love between Christ and the Church. Marriage is a sacrament precisely because it images the love of Christ and the Church, but unless love or the right to love is regarded as essential to marriage, then marriage is incapable of performing that imaging function, and without the imaging function there is no sacrament. To put it another way, how can a couple symbolize the love of Christ and the Church unless they pledge to love one another?

Finally, a fifth reason is that marital consent, as defined in canon 1057, §2, is, as Urban Navarrete said, "essentially an act of love."[22] The canon says that "matrimonial consent is an act of the will by which a man and a woman, through an irrevocable covenant, mutually give and accept each other [*sese mutuo tradunt et accipiunt*] in order to establish marriage."

The canon, it should be noted, does not say simply that the parties mutually *give* themselves to each other. Rather it seems to go out of its way (as did *Gaudium et spes*) to state quite exactly that parties "mutually *give and accept* each other" which, as we have seen, is precisely what love is. It seems quite clear, therefore, that, according to canon 1057, what the parties consent to at the time of marriage is to love each other.

So much for a brief statement of the position. Let us look now at some possible objections.

D. Some Objections

1. A first objection to love ever being regarded as essential to marriage is that Pope Paul VI, in his allocution to the Rota on February 9, 1976,[23] seemed to indicate that that can never be the case. Pope Paul took issue, in that allocution, with those people who "consider conjugal love as an element of such great importance in law . . . that they subordinate to it the very validity of the marriage bond" and he also noted that "conjugal love is not included in the province of law."

   When, however, the entire allocution is read, it is clear that there is no real conflict between the position of Paul VI and the position taken in this paper. Paul was making the point that it is consent and only consent that makes marriage, and once that consent is given an indissoluble bond is created. Whether the parties are in love prior to marriage or whether they fall out of love afterwards is juridically irrelevant.

   That, of course, is entirely true but in no way does it differ from our position. Our position does not claim that love is essential to marriage. Rather it claims first that *the right* to the *bonum coniugum* is part of the essential object of marital consent, and second that the *bonum coniugum* consists not in partnership, companionship, caring, etc., but rather in the love of the parties for each other.

   Once, however, the parties consent to marry and pledge to love each other, the marriage is then valid; it remains valid, of course, even if their commitment to love later disappears.

2. Another objection to our position is that whatever is consented to in marriage must be under the control of the will; love, however, is an affection or an emotion and, as such, is not under the control of the will. This is a point made by Bishop Zenon Grocholewski, Secretary of the Signatura, in his 1979 *Periodica* article.[24] How, he asks, can people oblige themselves to be affectionate? Either we are affectionate or we are not. We cannot just decide to be affectionate and then be so. Human nature does not work that way.

St. Thomas, however, states quite clearly that human nature in fact does work that way. Thomas takes up the question in several places[25] and he concludes that love may be viewed as residing either in the sensitive appetite or in the rational appetite. Even when it is in the sensitive appetite, however, love is under the command of the will. Thomas concludes, in other words, that a person's love is free and voluntary and can, indeed, even be measured. He notes, for example, that a man should love his wife more intensely than he does his parents, but he should love his parents with greater reverence than he does his wife.

It would seem, therefore, at least according to Thomistic psychology, that love *is* subject to the will and can therefore be something that is consented to in marriage. There is nothing inappropriate about spouses committing themselves, at the time of marriage, to being loving persons.

3. In that same 1979 article Bishop Grocholewski made another point which would certainly contradict my own position, so let me list that as objection three.

Grocholewski first of all recognizes that the *ius ad amorem* is essential for a valid marriage. For him, however, the essential nucleus of love is not love as we have defined it, namely as an affective tendency which is dialogical in nature. For Grocholewski, the essential nucleus of love includes no affectivity and no receiving, but only giving, non-affective giving.[26] By love, in other words, he means, if I understand him correctly, benevolence or, at the very most, caring (though he does not use that word). When people marry, according to Grocholewski, they give each other the right to benevolent acts and to a benevolent disposition, that and nothing more.

I would answer that objection, I think, by briefly recapping my earlier remarks about benevolence or goodwill. Benevolence, as Aquinas noted, is not love and it should not therefore be dignified with the title of love. Grocholewski calls benevolence love by confusing, as I see it, *benevolentia* with *amor benevolentiae*, which, as I tried to point out earlier, are two entirely different things. Benevolence, indeed, is not even friendship but only the *principium amicitiae*. In itself benevolence is an impersonal thing. It would seem, therefore, that benevolence by itself could not constitute the essential element of the *bonum coniugum,* which is generally regarded today not just as an interpersonal relationship but as an interpersonal relationship of some intimacy.

4. This brings me to the fourth objection and it is this. The 1983 Code of Canon Law studiously avoided incorporating Vatican II's well known description of marriage as an "intimate community of life and love." The studious avoidance of the phrase strongly suggests that the legislator found notions like intimacy and love to be unacceptable or unworkable within a legal framework. It suggests, in other words, that love might be grand in real life but that it has no legal relevancy and is out of place in a legal setting.

    This objection first of all smacks of legal positivism in that it implies that the written law is all important, certainly more important than justice or what is right and suitable for the community. But beyond that the fact is, I think, that the code simply wanted to leave the issue open. If it had included Vatican II's phrase, then it would at least to a large extent have closed off discussion; we would all be expected to accept the essentiality of love to marriage. Clearly, however, the world of canon law was not ready to do that in 1983, nor is it in 1986. The whole subject needs lots more thought and discussion. But the point is that we should not read more into the code's non-inclusion of the phrase than it merits. It means only that the subject is open to development, or non-development—through jurisprudence, books, articles, and so forth.

5. One last objection is the one proposed by Monsignor Palazzini in his Rotal decision of June 2, 1971, namely that if love were regarded as essential, how would jurists ever figure out what degree of love would have to be lacking before nullity would result? Would nullity result from a partial lack of love or only from a total lack? Would the defect have to be absolute or might relative suffice? How severe would the limitation have to be on the intensity of love before it would result in nullity? These, said Palazzini, are the "absurd consequences" of recognizing love as essential to marriage, and they demonstrate how illogical such a position is.[27]

    The point is well taken but perhaps exaggerated. On almost all grounds, after all, judgment calls are needed. That is what judges are for. In a force and fear case, for example, how much force is required before nullity results? In a *contra bonum prolis* case, how intense must the contraceptive intent be before it is considered to have prevailed over the marriage covenant? In a lack of due discretion case, how much discretion is "due" discretion? And so forth.

    If the *ius ad amorem* comes to be regarded as essential to marriage it will no doubt be difficult for judges at first. But a sound jurisprudence will soon develop and we will soon be able to make reasonable judgments about what it means exactly when we say that, in order to enter a valid marriage, the parties must intend to be loving spouses to each other.

E. Practical Implications

If the *ius ad amorem,* the right to a loving relationship came to be accepted as essential, the implications for jurisprudence would, I suppose, be rather obvious. Basically it would mean that the three grounds of lack of due competence, lack of due discretion, and simulation would all be expanded by one notch. If a person were judged to have lacked the capacity at the time of marriage to be a loving person to his or her spouse, that person would be considered to have lacked due competence. Or if a party did not maturely evaluate and freely accept love as one of the essential rights and duties of marriage, that person would lack due discretion. Or if, finally, a party excluded by a positive act of the will the *ius ad bonum coniugum* (having love as its essential ingredient), then that person would simulate marriage.

But even beyond the somewhat narrow tribunal implications of this position, there is also a broader implication here; it would bring into harmony the *lex orandi* and the *lex credendi*. In *Mediator Dei* (nn. 46-48) Pius XII warned against possible abuses of the "lex orandi, lex credendi" axiom but he also noted that the liturgy is very definitely a "locus theologicus" and a legitimate criterion of faith. The liturgy, in short, is a teacher of doctrine.

There is no question, it seems to me, but that the marriage liturgy (the prayers of the wedding Mass and the wedding rite itself) portrays love not just as important to marriage, but as essential to it. Love is at the core of the wedding liturgy. The wedding rings are said to be a sign of the bride and groom's love and fidelity, and throughout the ceremony God is implored over and over again to bless their love and to make them one in their love for each other. Furthermore, canon 1063, 3° (a very significant canon, it seems to me) specifically notes that the wedding liturgy should clarify "that the spouses signify and share in that mystery of unity and fruitful love that exists between Christ and the Church."

If, therefore, the *ius ad amorem* came to be generally recognized in law as essential to marriage, then law and liturgy (not to mention sacramentology) would finally come together, and that, it seems to me, is right and just, *dignum*, and above all, *iustum*.

ENDNOTES

[1] A. C. Jemolo, *Il Matrimonio nel Diritto Canonico* (Milano: Casa Editrice Dr. Francesco Vallardi, 1941), p. 76.

[2] *S R R Dec.* 61 (1969) 184. For an English translation see Lawrence G. Wrenn, *Decisions,* 1st ed. (Toledo: CLSA, 1980), p. 100. See also Thomas Aquinas, *ST,* Suppl. Q. 41, a. 1, especially ad 3; Q. 42, a. 2 and Q. 65, a. 2.

[3] *ST,* II^a^-II^ae^, Q. 27, a. 2, *sed contra.*

[4] C. S. Lewis, *The Four Loves* (New York: Harcourt-Brace-Jovanovich, 1960), pp. 95-96.

[5] *CLD* 8: 778-781, under VI, a.

[6] *ST,* II^a^-II^ae^, Q. 27, a. 2, obj. 3

[7] Lewis, pp 91-92.

[8] Milton Mayeroff, *On Caring* (New York: Harper and Row, 1971), p. 8

[9] Rollo May, *Love and Will* (New York: W. W. Norton, 1969), p. 290.

[10] Martin Heidegger, *Being and Time* (New York: Harper and Row, 1962), p. 242.

[11] Mary McDermott Shideler, *The Theology of Romantic Love* (New York: Harper and Brothers, 1962), pp. 36-37.

[12] *ST*, I^a-II^{ae}, Q. 22-28.

[13] Ibid., Q. 26, a. 1.

[14] Ibid., Q. 26, a. 2.

[15] Ibid., Q. 28, a. 3.

[16] Ibid., Q. 28, a. 1.

[17] Ibid., Q. 26, a. 4.

[18] Karl Rahner, *Theological Dictionary* (New York: Herder and Heder, 1965), p. 266.

[19] Shideler, p. 126.

[20] *ST*, I^a-II^{ae}, Q. 28, a, 1.

[21] Theodore Mackin, *What Is Marriage?* (New York: Paulist Press, 1982), pp. 332 ff.

[22] Urbanus Navarrete, "Structura Iuridica Matrimonii Secundum Concilium Vaticanum II," *Periodica* 57 (1968) 208.

[23] *CLD* 8: 790-795.

[24] Zenon Grocholewski, "De 'communione vitae' in novo schemate 'de matrimonio' et de momento iuridico amoris coniugalis," *Periodica* 68 (1979(474.

[25] *ST*, I^a, Q. 83, a. 1; I^a-II^{ae}, Q. 6, a. 8; Q. 17, a. 7; Q. 24, a. 1; Q. 26, a. 1 and 2; Q, 28 a. 3; and II^a-II^{ae}, Q. 26, a. 11.

[26] Grocholewski, p. 469.

[27] *SRR Dec.* 63 (1971) 471.

APPENDIX THREE

The Value Of Presumptions

It is well known that Canon 1608 requires a judge to be morally certain of the invalidity of a marriage before he can render an affirmative decision. Pope Pius XII, in his celebrated allocution of 1942, gave great prominence to the requirement of moral certitude and clearly distinguished it from probability. And Defenders of the Bond are forever reminding judges that Canon 1608 is one of the more inspired canons of the Code. It has, in other words, been literally drilled into us that invalidity must be proved beyond the shadow of a doubt or it is not proved at all. Certitude is sanity; probability is a miss and a miss is as good as a mile.

What value, then, will a judge attach to a presumption, which is, by definition, something which is probable and uncertain? A presumption, please note, is not something which is just probable *or* just uncertain. It is both at the same time. The Code defines a presumption as "a probable conjecture about an uncertain matter."[1]

Is it possible, then, that something so thoroughly probable and uncertain could ever result in certitude?

Bartocetti thinks not. He says:

> The only presumptions which a judge can call upon are those which are *outside* the law; he may not use those which are *against* the law; that is to say, a judge may not make up presumptions which disagree with those presumptions already stated in the law.
>
> This is a very important point: namely that against the presumption of Canon 1014 (which says that a marriage that was certainly celebrated must be presumed valid) a contrary *presumption* cannot be admitted but only contrary *proof* or those presumptions which are called vehement and which are equivalent to proof. Likewise, against the presumption of Canon 1086, 1 (which says that the internal consent of the parties is presumed to conform to the external expression of it) only positive arguments are admitted, not presumptions. All of which should be evident. Because there would be no point in the law stating presumptions if any judge could come along and overrule them with presumptions of his own.[2]

It is *not* entirely clear on what grounds Bartocetti objects to classifying presumptions as proofs. It is surely not simply because no presumption taken alone results in certitude since according to this criterion even the testimony of witnesses would be disqualified.

But it is entirely clear that for Bartocetti proof and presumption are two entirely different things. The only presumption Bartocetti would acknowledge as constituting proof would be what is called a vehement presumption. A vehement presumption, however, is not really a presumption at all. It is not, at least, what the Code means by a presumption.

Presumptions, in the wide sense of the term, can be of three kinds: vehement, grave and light. A *vehement* presumption constitutes full proof and results in certitude. For example, finding a man and woman naked in bed together results in a vehement presumption of intercourse. A *grave* presumption constitutes a semifull proof and in itself results only in probability. For example, a man seen slinking out of a house of prostitution in the wee hours would be gravely presumed to have enjoyed the hospitality of one of the tenants. Finally, a *light* presumption constitutes no proof at all and results in a mere suspicion. For example, a man seen talking to a pretty young woman cannot legitimately be presumed guilty of anything even slightly immoral.

Of these three, only the grave qualifies as a presumption according to the definition given in the Code of Canon Law, namely "a probable conjecture about an uncertain matter." The vehement is *more* than a probable conjecture. It is a certain conclusion. And the light is *less* than a probable conjecture. It is a rash suspicion.

A *vehement* presumption is really not so much a presumption as a jurisprudential interpretation. When Canestri, for example, says that a tenacious and perpetual intention to exclude cohabitation results in a vehement presumption favoring simulation,[3] he is not so much conjecturing about the invalidity of the marriage as he is stating what must be proved for the marriage to be invalid.

A *light* presumption, on the other hand, really amounts to what is known in jurisprudence as an indication (indicium), often referred to as circumstantial evidence. There are, in other words, lots of circumstances (e.g. the fact that a couple doesn't love each other, that they fight constantly and are unfaithful to each other shortly after the marriage) from which one could not legitimately presume invalidity but which are nevertheless extremely important for a judge to note.

It should probably be mentioned in passing that the term "indication" is rather muddled in jurisprudence. Schmalzgrueber[4] understood it to mean the external sign from which a presumption arose, as though the indication were something objective and the presumption subjective. The Instruction *Provida Mater,* on the other hand, seemed to equivalate indications and presumptions when it entitled the section *De Indiciis SEU Praesumptionibus* but Doheny, in his *Canonical Procedure in Matrimonial Cases*[5] skirted this problem by translating the heading "Indications AND Presumptions." But having taken note of the confusion in terminology, it may still be said that generally speaking an indication refers to some minor but not unimportant circumstance which would not support a real presumption or by itself result in even probable proof but which nevertheless might shed real light on the case. When a particular circumstance *does* support a grave presumption, it should not be referred to as an indication but rather a presumption.

At any rate, it is precisely this grave presumption (or what may simply be referred to as a presumption) which Bartocetti distinguishes from a proof and which he says may not be used to support invalidity. Nevertheless, Bartocetti notwithstanding, a presumption *is* certainly a proof and beyond doubt can and should be used against the presumptions of law favoring validity.

This is evident first and foremost from the fact that in the structure of the Code, the chapter on presumptions is found under Part II, Title IV — Concerning Proofs, so that, according to the axiom "A rubris ad nigrum valet illatio," the Code considers a presumption as a proof. Perhaps this was a disputed point before the 1917 Code but once that Code was published, it was no longer debatable. A presumption is certainly a proof.

The point is further made by Grazioli and Canestri in the two following, rather illuminating excerpts from sentences given in 1935 and 1940:

> If there is no violent presumption operative, full proof can nevertheless be obtained from other indications and circumstances. On this matter, Reiffenstuel notes, 'A presumption of man which is reasonable and probable only results in semifull proof, but if it is supported by the good reputation of the deponent and other circumstantial evidence, it can even result in full proof.'[6]

> In order to gain moral certitude about the matter under consideration in accord with Canon 1869, 1-3, a judge ought to base his argument not only on those reasons which in themselves result in full proof; but he may also acquire certitude with the help of presumptions, indications and circumstances all taken together, that is to say, with the help of those things which complete incomplete or semifull proof. For in moral matters (as opposed to certain abstract sciences) the sum of many arguments, which taken individually are only more or less probable, can result in certitude. All of which is recognized and accepted in our jurisprudence.[7]

In a given case it is, of course, for the judge to decide whether this presumption is more or less grave than that one or whether this presumption plus this or that indication is sufficient to establish proof. There are no general rules. Each presumption must be decided in its own context. Nevertheless, it can be instructive, if only by way of illustration, to examine some of the presumptions commonly accepted in jurisprudence. Such presumptions might gain or lose a little weight in a different set of circumstances but they will always have at least the same general effect of establishing semifull proof.

Perhaps the best known of the presumptions in marital jurisprudence is that of aversion in the force and fear case. In literally hundreds of cases, the Rota has affirmed the principle that in a force and fear case aversion establishes a presumption of nullity. Janasik, for example, said, "A grave juridic presumption of a forced marriage arises from the proved aversion of the one who is afraid."[8] Aversion is commonly known as the "indirect proof" in a force and fear case[9] and takes its strength as an argument from the fact that when one party marries reluctantly and "against his will," the logical assumption is that the will was forced.[10]

True aversion, in other words, results in semifull proof of nullity in a force and fear case. But it must be, as Heard says, *true* aversion and not just lack of love, "for people frequently, easily and for a variety of reasons, enter a marriage without love but this does not establish any kind of presumption favoring forced consent."[11] On the other hand, true aversion plus other circumstances can result in more than semifull proof. On March 20, 1942, for example, Grazioli decided the very interesting case of Joseph and Emily. This was a case loaded down with circumstantial evidence. The engagement had been broken and Joseph was in love with another woman. The marriage took place secretly and at night, in a foreign state and with fraudulent documents, etc., etc. And Grazioli decided that the presumption arising from Joseph's aversion plus the strange circumstances resulted in moral certitude of nullity. No further proof was required.[12]

So much for the force and fear case. Another interesting field for presumptions is the area of the intention against children or fidelity. In the early 1940s, Canestri issued a series of decisions in which he indicated that in such cases, four presumptions are operative, namely, condition, pact, perpetuity and tenacity.[13]

The first two, condition and pact, Canestri always regarded as the more weighty and by 1945 he was referring to them as vehement presumptions. Canestri himself always understood these terms in their strict sense and, so understood, they are indeed vehement presumptions, for these terms mean nothing else than an intrinsic limitation of marital consent. They are simply different ways of expressing the phrase "invalidating intention." They are synonyms or equivalencies in jurisprudence, so that, as Staffa noted, they are not really presumptions at all but rather constitute certain proof, or better, constitute what has to be proved.[14]

The other two presumptions, namely perpetuity and tenacity, Canestri originally referred to more as indications than anything else but later he referred to them as "not very weighty presumptions" or as "rather weak presumptions, bordering on indications," but presumptions nonetheless. With the passage of time, however, *perpetuity* has come to be regarded as a presumption of average strength and *tenacity* as more or less strong, depending on the degree of tenacity.

To these two presumptions (condition and pact, as we have seen, should not really be classified as presumptions) it would seem that one more could be added, namely, *cause*. A cause, as is well known, is not a condition attached to the marriage, but rather a motive for the marriage. And where a man, for example, is marrying a woman because she has agreed to postpone children for a couple of years, it seems reasonable to consider this as at least a borderline presumption favoring nullity. If, in other words, the man would not have married the woman if she had not agreed to postpone children (i.e. the effect would not have occurred had the cause not been present) then the postponement of children must have been very important to him, probably, that is to say, presumably, important enough for it to have invaded the heart of the covenant and so invalidated the marriage. Cause, in short, is a kind of prematrimonial tenacity.

A simple agreement by both parties to abuse marriage doesn't really prove or even semiprove anything. It does not constitute a presumption. Heard notes, "Fairly often, especially these days, a couple might intend to enter a real marriage but at the same time, for reasons of expediency, agree to avoid having children, without in any way making that a part of marital consent or restricting consent in any way."[15]

But it is one thing for a couple to decide to postpone children and quite another for one party to decide to marry only after he determines that the other party agrees to postpone children. This latter situation, much more than the former, warrants a legitimate conjecture regarding the centrality or the intrinsicality of the limitation.

Furthermore, it is one thing to marry because the other party will become a Catholic and quite another because the other party agrees to avoid children at least for a while. The former is a "simple cause," the latter is a "qualified cause," that is, it is directly relevant to the alleged grounds of nullity and demonstrates, though incompletely, the intimate relationship of the offspring issue to the marriage covenant in the mind of the alleged simulator.

There are, therefore, three presumptions: cause, perpetuity and tenacity, which may be utilized in cases of alleged intentions against children and fidelity.

A third area in which presumptions play an important part is the case of simple error about the indissolubility of marriage as it relates to an intention against perpetuity. Canon 1099 says that error about the perpetuity of marriage does not vitiate marital consent unless it determines the will but several Rotal decisions have said that when the error is deeply ingrained and intense or when there is added to the error a certain reluctance to marry, then a presumption arises favoring invalidity. Canestri even notes, "The deeper the error, the stronger the presumption, for who can conceive of a man adhering to some opinion with great obstinacy and then deflecting from it when it comes to action."[16]

These are but a few examples of the value of presumptions in judging marriage cases. As Pope Pius XII said in his allocution of 1942:

> Sometimes moral certainty is derived only from an aggregate of indications and proofs which, taken singly, do not provide the foundation for true certitude, but which, when taken together, no longer leave room for any reasonable doubt on the part of a man of sound judgment. This is in no sense a passage from probability to certainty through a simple cumulation of probabilities, which would amount to an illegitimate transit from one species to another essentially different one; it is rather to recognize that the simultaneous presence of all these separate indications and proofs can have a sufficient basis only in the existence of a common origin or foundation from which they spring, that is, in objective truth and reality. In this case, therefore, certainty arises from the wise application of a principle which is absolutely secure and universally valid, namely the principle of a sufficient reason. Consequently, if in giving the reasons for his decision, the judge

states that the proofs which have been adduced, considered separately, cannot be judged sufficient, but that, taken together and embraced in a survey of the whole situation, they provide the necessary elements for arriving at a safe definitive judgment, it must be acknowledged that such reasoning is in general sound and legitimate.

ENDNOTES

[1] C. 1584
[2] *De Causis Matrimonialibus,* p. 194.
[3] S.R.R.D. 39, 8.
[4] *Ius Ecclesiasticum,* Vol. 4, p. 212.
[5] Vol. I, p. 413.
[6] S.R.R.D. 27, 266.
[7] S.R.R.D. 32, 325.
[8] S.R.R.D. 28, 450.
[9] See, for example, S.R.R.D. 49, 216.
[10] S.R.R.D. 34, 672.
[11] S.R.R.D. 36, 692.
[12] S.R.R.D. 34, 214.
[13] S.R.R.D. 33, 695 and 877; 34, 312; 35, 905; 37, 268 and 365.
[14] S.R.R.D. 41, 462.
[15] S.R.R.D. 37, 401.
[16] S.R.R.D. 30, 610.

APPENDIX FOUR

Private Response On Canon 1098

Issued by the Code Commission - February 8, 1986

Prot. No. 843/86

Your Excellency:

By letter of March 23, 1985, under protocol number 485/86, Your Excellency was informed that the question posed by you to the Supreme Tribunal of the Apostolic Signatura regarding the possible retroactivity of Canon 1098 of the Code of Canon Law was, for reasons of competence, transferred to this dicastery and was under study by this Pontifical Commission.

I would like now to assure you that the question, after first being subjected to a special and profound study by several of our consultors, was then examined collegially in a Consultation held on December 13 of last year in which it was decided, given the doctrinal complexity of the question, to have the matter placed before a Plenarium of the Cardinal Fathers of the Commission who would decide on the opportuneness of giving an authentic interpretation in this matter.

The Consultation is inclined to regard the wording of Canon 1098 as of merely positive law and consequently as *nonretroactive*. Given, however, the great variety of cases which the canon could embrace, one could not a priori rule out the possibility that some of those cases could involve nullity deriving from the natural law, in which case it would be legitimate to render an affirmative decision. It is therefore the task of the judge, who is in possession of all the possible facts, to determine whether the case at bar involves a type of error invalidating the consent not by the positive disposition of Canon 1098 but by force of the natural law, as was the case in certain sentences that predated the promulgation of the Code.

To arrive finally at a clarification and investigation of these criteria and concepts is a task reserved to doctrine.[1] In spite of the risk that meanwhile there will be different doctrinal interpretations and therefore different judicial decisions, it still seems inappropriate to preempt the doctrinal task by an authentic canonical interpretation. At any rate, it will, as I have said, be incumbent upon the Plenarium to decide on the opportuneness of a decision clarifying the matter, a decision regarded by some as premature since a sufficient doctrinal investigation has not yet been conducted.

In the absence of an authentic interpretation which favors the nonretroactivity of Canon 1098, there obviously remains a doubt about the nature of the prescript of Canon 1098—and consequently a doubt about whether the canon may or may not be applied to marriages celebrated before November 27, 1983. In view of this doubt one should, of course, keep in mind Canon 1060 which indicates that "in doubt the validity of a marriage is to be upheld."

Trusting that these observations will be of some use to Your Excellency, I am

Devotedly yours,

Rosalio Cardinal Castillo Lara
President

J. Herranz
Secretary

[1] Translator's Note: A definitive decision on this matter would presumably be issued not by the Code Commission but by the Congregation for the Doctrine of the Faith, as in the case of the Decree of May 13, 1977 regarding impotence. See D2, pp. 1-2.

SELECTIVE BIBLIOGRAPHY

Reference Works

American Handbook of Psychiatry. Ed. by Silvano Arieti. Vols., 1-2. New York: Basic Books, Inc., 1959, Vol. 3, 1966.

Bartocetti, Victorius. *De Causis Matrimonialibus.* Romae: 1950.

Bogdan, Leonard A. *Renewal of Consent in The Simple Convalidation of Marriage.* Dissertation Excerpt, Rome, Pontificia Università Lateranense, 1979.

Brenkle, John J. *The Impediment of Male Impotence with Special Application to Paraplegia.* Washington: Catholic University, 1963.

Diagnostic and Statistical Manual of Mental Disorders. Washington: American Psychiatric Association. First edition 1952. Second edition 1968. Third edition 1980. Third edition revised 1987.

Documenta Recentiora Circa Rem Matrimonialem et Processualem, Vol. I edited by I. Gordon and Z. Grocholewski, Rome 1977; Vol. II, edited by Z. Grocholewski, 1980.

Documentation on Marriage Nullity Cases. First compilation by Germain Lesage and Francis Morrisey, Ottawa, St. Paul University 1971; Second compilation by J. Edward Hudson, 1979.

Doyle, Thomas P. editor, *Marriage Studies,* CLSA,, Vol. I, 1980, Vol. II, 1982, Vol. III, 1985.

Fellhauer, David E. *The Consortium Omnis Vitae as A Juridical Element of Marriage,* Ottawa, University of St. Paul, 1979 (Vol. 13, n. 1, of Studia Canonica).

Frattin, Peter L. *The Matrimonial Impediment of Impotence: Occulusion of Spermatic Ducts and Vaginismus.* Washington: Catholic University, 1958.

Freedman, Alfred with Harold Kaplan and Benjamin Sadock. *Comprehensive Textbook of Psychiatry - II,* 2 vols., Baltimore: The Williams and Wilkins Company, 1975.

Grocholewski, Zenon. *De Exclusione Indissolubilitatis ex Consensu Matrimoniali Eiusque Probatione.* Naples: D'Auria, 1973.

Häring, Bernard. *Marriage in the Modern World.* Westminster: The Newman Press, 1966.

Hastings, Donald. *Impotence and Frigidity.* New York: Delta, 1966.

Holböck, Carolus. *Tractatus De Iurisprudentia Sacrae Romane Rotae.* Graz: Styria, 1957.

Hudson, J. Edward. *Handbook for Marriage Nullity Cases.* Ottawa: St. Paul University, First edition 1975; Second edition 1980.

Keating, John Richard. *The Bearing of Mental Impairment on the Validity of Marriage.* Roma: Gregorian University Press, 1964.

Lazzarato, Damianus. *Iurisprudentia Pontificia - De Metu.* Typis Polyglottis Vaticanis: 1956.

----------- *Iurispurdentia Pontificia - De Causis Matrimonialibus Praeter Metum.* 3 Vols., Neapoli: M. D'Auria, 1963.

Mackin, Theodore. *What is Marriage?* New York, Paulist Press, 1982.

Masters, William H. and Virginia E. Johnson. *Human Sexual Inadequacy.* Boston: Little, Brown and Company, 1970.

Matrimonial Jurisprudence, United States. 5 Vols. covering years 1968-1976. Toledo: CLSA, published annually beginning 1973.

Mendonca, Augustine. *Antisocial Personality and Nullity of Marriage.* Ottawa: University of St. Paul, 1982. (Vol. 16, n. 1 of Studia Canonica).

Navarrette, Urbanus. *Structura Iuridica Matrimonii Secundum Concilium Vaticanum II: Momentum iuridicum amoris coniugalis.* Roma: Pontificia Università Gregoriana, 1968.

Netter, Frank H. *The Ciba Collection of Medical Illustrations. Reproductive System.* Summit, New Jersey: Ciba, 1954.

Noonan, John T. Jr. *Power to Dissolve.* Cambridge: The Belknap Press, 1972.

Orsy, Ladislas. *Marriage in Canon Law.* Wilmington, Michael Glazier, 1986.

Pospishil, Victor J. *Divorce and Remarriage.* New York: Herder and Herder, 1967.

Sable, Robert M., coordinator and editor. *Incapacity For Marriage: Jurisprudence and Interpretation,* Acts of the III Gregorian Colloquium. Rome: Pontificia Universitas Gregoriana, 1987.

Schillebeeckx, E. *Marriage: Human Reality and Saving Mystery.* New York: Sheed and Ward, 1965.

Staffa, Dinus. *De Conditione Contra Matrimonii Substantiam.* Romae: Libraria Pont. Instituti Utriusque Iuris, 1955.

The Bond of Marriage. Ed. by William Bassett. University of Notre Dame Press, 1968.

The Future of Marriage as Institution. Ed. by Franz Böckle. New York: Herder and Herder, Volume 55 of the Concilium Series, 1970.

The Tribunal Reporter. Ed. by Adam J. Maida. Huntington: Our Sunday Visitor Inc., 1970.

Tobin, William J. *Homosexuality and Marriage.* Rome: Catholic Book Agency, 1964.

Understanding Alcoholism. New York: Charles Scribner's Sons, 1968.

Van Ommeren, William M. *Mental Illness Affecting Matrimonial Consent* (Canon Law Studies #415). Washington, D.C.: Catholic University of America Press, 1961.

Wrenn, Lawrence G. *Decisions.* Washington, D.C., CLSA, First edition, 1980. Second edition 1983.

Articles

Ahern, Maurice B. "The Marital Right to Children: A Tentative Reexamination. *Studia Canonica.* 8, 1974, pp. 91-107.

---------- "Error and Deception as Grounds for Nullity." *Studia Canonica.* 11, 1977, pp. 225-259.

Arena, Aldo. "The Jurisprudence of the Sacred Roman Rota: Its Development and Direction After the Second Vatican Council." *Studia Canonica.* 12, 1978, pp. 265-293.

Bauer, Francis, M.D. "Relative Incapacity to Establish a Christian Conjugal Union." *CLSA Proceedings.* 1974, pp. 36-44.

Bernhard, Jean. "The Evolution of Matrimonial Jurisprudence: The Opinion of a French Canonist." *The Jurist.* 41, 1981, pp. 105-116.

Bogdan, Leonard A. "Simple Convalidation of Marriage in the 1983 Code of Canon Law." *The Jurist* 46, 1986, pp. 511-531.

Bolen, Darrell W. "Gambling and Sex." *Medical Aspects of Human Sexuality.* May, 1969, pp. 60-65.

Braceland, Francis J. "Psychoneurotic Interpersonal Reaction: Incompatibility and the Tribunal." *CLSA Proceedings.* 1970, 63-70.

---------- "Schizophrenic Remissions." *The Jurist.* XXI. pp. 362-374.

Brown, Ralph. "Inadequate Consent or Lack of Commitment: Authentic Grounds for Nullity." *Studia Canonica.* 9, 1975, pp. 249-265.

---------- "Total Simulation - A Second Look." *Studia Canonica.* 10, 1976, pp. 235-249.

---------- "Non Inclusion: A Form of Simulation?" CLSA *Proceedings.* 1979, pp. 1-11.

---------- "Essential Incompatibility: Researches and the Present Situation." *Studia Canonica.* 14, 1980, pp. 25-48.

---------- "Simulation versus Lack of Commitment." *Studia Canonica.* 14, 1980, pp. 335-345.

Burke, Raymond L. "Canon 1095: Canonical Doctrine and Jurisprudence. Part I: Canon 1095, 1° and 2°." *CLSA Proceedings.* 1986, pp. 94-107.

Cavanagh, John R. "Sexual Anomalies and the Law." *The Catholic Lawyer.* Vol. 9, No. 1. Winter, 1963, pp. 4-31.

Coburn, Vincent P. "Homosexuality and the Invalidation of Marriage." *The Jurist.* XX. 1960, pp. 441-459.

Cuneo, J. James. "Lack of Due Discretion: The Judge as Expert." *The Jurist*. 42, 1982, pp. 141-163.

---------- "Deceit/Error of Person as a *Caput Nullitatis.*" *CLSA Proceedings*, 1983, pp. 154-166.

Cunningham, Richard. "Recent Rotal Decisions and Today's Marriage Theology: Nothing Has Changed - Or Has It?" *CLSA Proceedings*. 1976, pp. 24-41.

Curran, Charles E. "Divorce: Catholic Theory and Practice in the United States." *The American Ecclesiastical Review*. 1974, pp. 3-34 and 75-95.

De Luca, Luigi. "The New Law on Marriage." *The New Code of Canon Law: Proceedings of the 5th International Congress*, 1986, pp. 827-851.

Doyle, Thomas P. "A New Look at The Bonum Fidei." *Studia Canonica*. 12, 1978, pp. 5-40.

Felici, Pericle. "Juridical Formalities and Evaluation of Evidence in the Canonical Process." *The Jurist*. 38, 1978, pp. 153-157.

Fellhauer, David E. "The Exclusion of Indissolubility: Old Principles and New Jurisprudence." *Studia Canonica*. 9, 1975, pp. 105-133.

---------- "Psychological Incapacity for Marriage in the Revised *Code of Canon Law*." *The New Code of Canon Law: Proceedings of the 5th International Congress*, 1986, pp. 1019-1040.

---------- "Canon 1095: Canonical Doctrine and Jurisprudence, Part II: Canon 1095, 3°". *CLSA Proceedings*, 1986, pp. 107-117.

Finnegan, John T. "When Is A Marriage Indissoluble?" *The Jurist*. 28, 1968, pp. 309-329.

---------- "The Capacity to Marry." *The Jurist*. 29, 1969. 141-156.

Graham, George P. "Personality Disorders and Their Effect on the Validity of Marriage." *CLSA Proceedings*. 1976, pp. 138-149.

Graham, James J. "Transsexualism and the Capacity To Enter Marriage." *The Jurist*. 41, 1981, pp. 117-154.

Gramont, Ignatius and Wauk, Leroy A. "Capacity and Incapacity to Contract Marriage." *Studia Canonica*, 22, 1988, pp. 147-168.

Green, Richard, M.D. "Change of Sex." *Medical Aspects of Human Sexuality*. October, 1969, pp. 96-113.

Grenier, Henri. "Can We Still Speak of the Petrine Privilege?" *The Jurist*. 38. 1978, pp. 158-162.

Grocholewski, Zenon. "De 'Communione Vitae' in Novo Schemate 'De Matrimonio' et De Momento Iuridico Amoris Coniugalis." *Periodica*, 1979, 3, pp. 439-480.

---------- "Relatio Inter Errorem et Positivam Indissolubilitatis Exclusionem in Nuptiis Contrahendis." *Periodica*. 1980, 3-4, pp. 569-601.

Hudson, J. Edward. "Index of Selected Rotal Decisions, 1967-1975." *Studia Canonica*. 11, 1977, pp. 67-84.

Humphreys, John. "Lack of Commitment in Consent." *Studia Canonica*. 10, 1976, pp. 345-362.

Johnson, John G. "The Simple Convalidation As a Pastoral Problem." *Studia Canonica*. 15, 1981, pp. 461-479.

---------- "Ligamen and Multiple Marriages: Too Good To Be True?" *The Jurist*. 42, 1982, pp. 222-228.

Kafka, Franz. "In The Penal Colony." *The Penal Colony*. New York: Schocken Books. 1948, pp. 191-227.

Kaufman, Joseph J. "Urologic Factors in Impotence and Premature Ejaculation." *Medical Aspects of Human Sexuality*. September, 1967, pp. 43-48.

Keating, John Richard. "The Caput Nullitatis in Insanity Cases." *The Jurist*. 22, 1962, pp. 391-411.

---------- "Sociopathic Personality." *The Jurist*. 25, 1965, pp. 429-438.

Kelleher, Stephen J. "Canon 1014 and American Culture." *The Jurist*. 28, 1968, pp. 1-12.

---------- "The Problem of the Intolerable Marriage." *America*. September 14, 1968, pp. 178-182.

---------- "Catholic Annulments: A Dehumanizing Process." *Commonweal*. June 10, 1977, pp. 363-368.

Kennedy, Eugene C. "Signs of Life in Marriage." In *Divorce and Remarriage in the Catholic Church,* edited by L. G. Wrenn, New York: Newman, 1973.

Kenyon, Roger A. "The Nature and Nullity of Matrimonial Consent: Arguments Based on Primary Sources." *Studia Canonica.* 14, 1980, pp. 107-154.

Kinch, R. A. H. "Painful Coitus." *Medical Aspects of Human Sexuality.* October, 1967, pp. 6-12.

Lader, Malcom. "Valium and Associated Drugs Which Can Influence The Giving of True Matrimonial Consent." *Studia Canonica.* 13, 1979, pp. 455-464.

LaDue, William J. "The Ends of Marriage." *The Jurist.* 29, 1969, pp. 424-427.

---------- "The Sacramentality of Marriage." *CLSA Proceedings.* 1974, pp. 25-35.

---------- "Conjugal Love and The Juridical Structure of Christian Marriage." *The Jurist.* 34, 1974, pp. 36-67.

Lebel, Robert Roger. "Genetic Grounds For Annulment." *The Jurist.* 36, 1976, pp. 317-327.

Lesage, Germain. "The Consortium Vitae Coniugalis: nature and applications." *Studia Canonica.* 6, 1972, pp. 99-113.

Manning, Michael. "Essential Incompatibility: A Valid Ground of Nullity?" *Studia Canonica.* 13, 1979, pp. 339-362.

McGrath, Aidan. "On the Gravity of Causes of a Psychological Nature in the Proof of Inability to Assume the Essential Obligations of Marriage." *Studia Canonica.* 22, 1988, pp. 67-75.

Mendonca, Augustine. "Schizophrenia and Nullity of Marriage." *Studia Canonica.* 17, 1983, pp. 197-237.

---------- "The Effects of Personality Disorders on Matrimonial Consent." *Studia Canonica.* 21, 1987, pp. 67-123.

---------- "The Incapacity to Contract Marriage: Canon 1095." *Studia Canonica.* 19, 1985, pp. 259-325.

---------- "The Theological and Juridical Aspects of Marriage." *Studia Canonica.* 22, 1988, pp. 265-304

Miller, Ira. "The Don Juan Character." *Medical Aspects of Human Sexuality.* April, 1969, pp. 43-48.

Morrisey, Francis. "Proposed Legislation on Defective Matrimonial Consent." *CLSA Proceedings.* 1974, pp. 71-82.

---------- "The Impediment of Ligamen and Multiple Marriages." The Jurist. 40, 1980, pp. 406-418.

Navarrete, Urbano. "'Incapacitas assumendi onera' uti caput autonomum nullitatis matrimonii." *Periodica,* LXI. 1972, pp. 47-80.

---------- "De iure ad vitae communionem: observationes ad novum Schema canonis 1086 §2." *Periodica,* LXVI. 1977, pp. 249-270.

Newton, Michael. "The Artificial Vagina." *Medical Aspects of Human Sexuality.* December, 1968, pp. 28-31.

O'Neill, William P. "Towards An Understanding of the Marriages of Those in Law Enforcement." *Studia Canonica.* 13. 1979, pp. 403-427.

Orsy, Ladislas. "Matrimonial Consent in the New Code: *Glossae* on Canons 1057, 1095-1103, 1107. *The Jurist.* 43. 1983, pp. 29-68.

Reinhardt, Marion J. "Updating the Marriage Tribunal." *America.* November 9, 1968, pp. 429-433.

---------- "The Incidence of Mental Disorder." *Studia Canonica.* 6. 1972, pp. 209-225.

Ritty, Charles J. "Possible Invalidity of Marriage by Reason of Sexual Anomalies." *The Jurist.* 23, 1963, pp 394-422.

---------- "The Transsexual and Marriage." *Studia Canonica.* 15. 1981, pp. 441-459.

Robinson, Geoffrey. "Unresolved Questions in the Theology of Marriage." *The Jurist.* 43, 1983, pp. 69-102.

Sanson, Robert J. "Jurisprudence for Marriage: Based on Doctrine." *Studia Canonica.* 10, 1976. pp. 5-36.

Schumacher, William A. "The Importance of Interpersonal Relations in Marriage." *Studia Canonica.* 10, 1976, pp. 75-112.

Sohval, Arthur R. "Klinefelter's Syndrome." *Medical Aspects of Human Sexuality.* August, 1969, pp. 69-86.

Thomas, Paul K. "Marriage Annulments for Gay Men and Lesbian Women: New Canonical and Psychological Insights." *The Jurist.* 43, 1983, pp. 318-342.

Vann, Kevin. "*Dolus:* Canon 1098 of the Revised Code of Canon Law." *The Jurist.* 47, 1987, pp. 371-393.

Wrenn, Lawrence G. "Marriage and Cohabitation." *The Jurist.* 27, 1967, pp. 85-89.

---------- "Simple Error and the Indissolubility of Marriage." *The Jurist.* 28, 1968, pp. 84-88.

---------- "An Outline of a Jurisprudence on Sociopathy." *The Jurist.* 28, October, 1968, pp. 470-485.

---------- "Notes on Canonical Jurisprudence." *The Jurist.* 29, 1969, pp. 57-69.

---------- "Integration or Segregation of Grounds. *The Jurist.* 29, 1969, pp. 183-188.

---------- "Notes But Mostly Footnotes on Presumptions." *The Jurist.* 30, 1970, pp. 206-215.

---------- "Epilepsy and Marriage." *The Jurist.* 32, 1972, pp. 91-101.

---------- "Invalid Convalidation." *The Jurist.* 32, 1972, pp. 253-265.

---------- "A New Condition Limiting Marriage." *The Jurist.* 34, 1974, pp. 292-315.

---------- "The Canon Law of Marriage." *The New Catholic Encyclopedia,* Vol. 17. 1979, pp. 384-388.

---------- "Marriage Tribunals and the Expert." *The Bulletin of the National Guild of Catholic Psychiatrists.* 1979, pp. 53-68.

Zusy, James B. "Matrimonial Consent and Immaturity." *Studia Canonica.* 15, 1981, pp. 199-239.

Periodicals

Apollinaris, Rome, 1928 -

Canon Law Abstracts. Drygrange Melrose, 1959 -

Communicationes, Romae, 1969 -

Ephemerides Iuris Canonici. Romae,, 1945 -

The Jurist, Washington, D.C. 1941 -

Medical Aspects of Human Sexuality. New York, 1967 -

Monitor Ecclesiasticus, Romae, 1876 -

Periodica de Re Canonica et Morali. Bruges, 1920-1927; *Periodica de Re Morali, Canonica, Liturgica.* Bruges, 1920-1936 and Romae 1937 -

Studia Canonica. Ottawa, 1967 -

More complete bibliographies may be found in *Documenta Recentiora,* in Doyle, *Marriage Studies,* Vol. II, and in Hudson, *Handbook.*